FIGHT
FOR YOUR
DREAM

ELAINE H. SHARP

ACORN BOOKS
www.acornbooks.co.uk

This edition published in 2015 by
Acorn Books
www.acornbooks.co.uk

Acorn Books is an imprint of
Andrews UK Limited
www.andrewsuk.com

Copyright © 2015 Elaine Hazel Sharp

The right of Elaine Hazel Sharp to be identified as
the author of this work has been asserted by her in
accordance with the Copyright, Designs and Patents
Act 1988

All rights reserved. No part of this publication may be
reproduced, stored in or introduced into a retrieval
system, or transmitted, in any form, or by any means
(electronic, mechanical, photocopying, recording or
otherwise) without the prior written permission of the
publisher. Any person who does any unauthorised act
in relation to this publication may be liable to criminal
prosecution and civil claims for damages.

Contents

For my late Father-in-law
Bill Sharp
1930-2003
"I Miss You Dad"

For my late Sister
Sylvia
1955-2010
"You Are Free Forever"

To Marty and Georgie to whom I owe so much
"You created a new life for me, I'll never forget you"
To those who battled in vain R.I.P

Acknowledgements

This book is dedicated to my devoted husband Nigel to whom I owe my life. I would never have made it through without his unrelenting love, patience and support; many a lesser man would have walked away. To my mum and dad, Nigel's mum and dad and my loving sister Denise who were there for me in my darkest moments. Thank you for standing by me.

Thank you to Professor Andrew Shorthouse, my surgeon who saved my life with his expertise, and throughout all my treatments. Thank you to Professor Malcolm Reed for looking after me through my many infections. Thank you to Dr. Iman Azmy who has now taken on that task. Thank you to Professor T.C.Li. My gynaecologist. Thank you to Louise, my psychologist who became a friend but sadly lost her battle with breast cancer. Thanks to Brenda and Sue my breast care nurses who have given their time so freely. Thank you to Thornbury Hospital staff, especially on Mappin Ward, on the many occasions I have been an inpatient you have always treated me with care and understanding. Thank you to my many friends who have supported me through difficult times. Thank you to our dear friends Jane and Steve who have gone above and beyond the meaning of 'friendship' not only for me but for Nigel as well. Thank you to Dr. Norman Macaskill, Words cannot express the gratitude I feel for immeasurably improving my life. I truly believe that I wouldn't be here without you. And finally, thank you to Joy Whitehead, who took on the task of tirelessly editing my manuscript. My sincere thanks go out to everyone.

FIGHT
FOR YOUR
DREAM

Discovery

It was 9.55pm on Wednesday 23rd October 1997. Coronation Street had just gone to the commercial break, and I was laid in bed in Nigel's arms as was quite usual at that time of night. The international football match had pushed Coronation street later than the usual 7.30pm slot, so I wanted to catch up on my regular viewing of the soap, as it was a favourite of mine back in those days.

'That was painful,' I thought to myself as Nigel squeezed me closer to him. Without giving it a second thought I felt under my nightshirt and pressed my hand onto my left breast. A wave of panic washed over me as I thought about Carol and Jane. Carol had been a close friend of mine, and Jane was my brother-in-law's sister. Both of them had recently died from breast cancer. I shook my head trying to banish thoughts of the big C. Surely I must be mistaken. It can't be a lump. My boobs are too small to cause any problem.

The intro music of the second half of Corrie wasn't holding my attention. My mouth was dry and, as I glanced upwards to Nigel, he had sensed my unrest. 'What's the matter?' asked Nigel. 'Err, I'm sure it must be my imagination, but can you feel a lump here?' I said, pushing his hand toward my breast. I was still looking upwards, to see if I could read anything from his facial expressions, when my worst fear was confirmed; yes he could feel a lump. The colour was draining from his face when he said, 'We need to go to the doctor's tomorrow to get that checked out.' For the next few minutes we didn't speak to each other. We were each quiet with our own thoughts, but our minds were working overtime.

Corrie had passed us by. The music was dwindling, signalling the end of another episode; but neither of us noticed - we were just mulling over our discovery.

That night I felt restless, tossing and turning, thinking I would soon find a comfy spot to fall asleep; but I just couldn't settle. Nigel was the same, but when I whispered, 'Are you asleep?' there was no answer. I knew he was awake, but he was trying to be positive and make me think he was having a good night's sleep. He couldn't fool me though - I'd seen the look on his face!

The next morning Nigel had showered and was dressing when I awoke. I'd fallen asleep eventually, but now it was morning and I felt so tired. 'You need to ring the surgery at 9.00am to make an appointment,' said Nigel. 'Well, I've been thinking. I might hang fire for a few days to see if this thing disappears,' I answered. 'Women's boobs can be lumpy at certain times of the month and I don't want to cause a fuss if it's nothing'. Nigel turned around, buttoning his shirt, and said, 'No, you won't. You'll go today. Don't be ridiculous.'

The surgery was busy that morning. It was Thursday, and the surgery was closed every Thursday afternoon, so you could always guarantee a wait to see a doctor. Just my luck: Dr Poxon was running late, and the surgery had squeezed me in at the end of the morning session when I had explained my concerns over the phone that morning. Eventually my name was called over the speaker. I'd not seen this doctor before; she was a lady doctor and immediately she put me at ease.

After a brief chat she asked me to undress and lay on the bed, where she could examine me. Checking both my boobs she made no comment, but I couldn't read her facial expressions as I had done with Nigel the previous evening. Nigel was like an open book for me, but I'd never met this doctor before.

'Can you show me where you can feel the lump?' she quizzed.

'Oh, God,' I thought, 'she can't feel anything.' I felt such a fraud. At first I couldn't find the lump, which only last night felt so prominent. 'Yeah, it's here,' I said, almost feeling relieved that I hadn't imagined it. 'Oh yes, yes, Mmm'.

'Okay, you can get dressed now.' Hurriedly I slipped on my bra and shirt and pulled the curtain back. I plonked myself back on the chair opposite the doctor.

'Well, it's small, whatever it is. I don't think it's anything to worry about, but I don't mess about with breast lumps so I think you should see a consultant. I'll write you a referral letter for a Mr Shorthouse; he's a general surgeon and very good'.

I can't really remember much about the drive home: only the echo of the doctor's voice. Breast lump! General surgeon! It's small whatever it is. But I just had this awful gut feeling that this was going to be bad news.

On returning home the first person I rang was Nigel. He tried to sound positive but I sensed that he too was concerned and, although Nigel is the stronger of the two of us, I couldn't convince myself that this wasn't going to be a problem.

It was about 11.30am by this time, and normally I rang my mum and dad for their daily check up. This morning they beat me to it. I tried to sound normal and upbeat, but they must have sensed something was wrong. 'What's the matter, Elaine, is your back bad?' asked dad. 'No, it's okay,' I said, and continued to blurt out something about finding a little lump. Mum was then handed the phone, and she did her best to reassure me: 'It's probably nothing, love.'

Denise, my middle older sister, rang me about one hour later, quizzing me about what the lump felt like. 'Is it hard? Is it soft? Does it hurt?' Obviously, mum and dad had rung Denise for their own reassurance on their youngest daughter. On the other end of the phone Denise cringed when I described the lump as feeling like a 'hard pea'.

Denise worked at the Royal Hallamshire Hospital in Sheffield and, after going through the trauma of Jane's death six months earlier, she felt like it was déjà vu: all happening again. I rang Thornbury, where an appointment was made for me to see Mr Andrew Shorthouse the following Monday evening 6.30pm. 'That's it then,' I thought, 'countdown.'

I would say that, throughout my life, I've always been quite a competitive person, and have always tried hard to achieve. But nothing, absolutely nothing, could have prepared me for the fight and challenge that lay ahead.

A Hard Act to Follow

'That's my boy' Grandad Allen congratulates my Dad after winning his first 10 mile National in record time

I was born on the 11th October 1963 into a working class family. My dad worked in a local steel forge, and mum did cleaning jobs in our local area. I was the youngest of three daughters; Sylvia was eight when I entered the world, and Denise was four. Dad had a tough physical job, which meant he worked shifts - mornings, afternoons and nights on a three weekly basis; so mum was always around to make sure that dad had a hearty meal, depending on what shift he was working. When we came home from school, be it lunchtime or teatime, we always had a hot meal to tuck into as well. Although we were just a normal working class family, both mum and dad always made sure we lived well. We had our annual holiday every year in Blackpool, and stayed in the same guest house year upon year.

The one exceptional thing about our family was sport. For as long as I can remember, I used to run everywhere: up to the local corner shop on errands for mum, up to school, back home for lunch, back to school and home again, round to friends' houses, everywhere involved running! I remember one day, when I was at school, I forgot my ingredients for a cookery lesson. So I decided to go and see my year tutor to ask if I could go home during my fifteen minute break time to collect them. When he asked why I was so sure I could make it home and back, still within break time, I promptly answered, 'Well, you see, I'm a cross country runner, so I know I will be quick; I run home for lunch everyday and back again, and if you check the register, I've never been in trouble for being late.' I realised in later years why the wry grin came across my tutors face! Permission granted, so off I went and I was still back before break time ended! That was a three mile round trip in less than fifteen minutes!

So it's no surprise that, as soon as I was old enough, I joined the local Athletics Club, where like minded people would meet on Tuesday and Thursday evenings and Sunday mornings to train. By the time I had turned twelve, I realised that sprint events were not my forte. I was a very slim girl and did not have the power of the stockier girls who came out of the blocks like rockets. I had always enjoyed the freedom of distance running, so I spoke to dad and we decided that I needed a different coach if I wanted to run distance. Decision made, dad took me along to see John and Sheila Sherwood, who used to train at our local track with an athletic squad of their own. Anybody involved in athletics will be familiar with the name Sherwood. Sheila won a silver medal at the Tokyo Olympics in 1964 for the long jump, and John won the bronze medal four years later in Mexico for the 400m hurdles. That was the year that David Emery won the gold. I felt very proud when John Sherwood told me I could join them. I'd always been in awe of them when I was training with my sprinting squad, so to be a part of the Sherwood squad was truly awesome. Dad was my driving force and athletics hero, and sadly proved to be an impossible act to follow.

Spring Bank holiday Tuesday in Sheffield was always a big day on the city's sporting calendar. It was the local Star Walk, and hundreds of wannabe athletes would take part to claim the prestigious first place. The event was a twelve mile race walk through the city. No feeding stations were allowed then, not like today: just twelve gruelling miles of hard toil! On one of these particular Tuesdays, dad was watching the event with his mum and dad, brothers, new wife and hundreds of other people. He turned to his dad just after the leading man had passed them and said, 'I'm going to win this next year.' His dad, my granddad Allen, just laughed and said, 'You, you'll never win this.' That was all the encouragement dad needed. He joined the local 'Sheffield United Harriers', and the following year, 1947, dad made the race his own when he took first place in record time! This was just the tip of the iceberg for dad's future glory in the sport. Dad went on to take the race walking world by storm, winning national championships at every distance, most of which were in record time. Dad took the sport to new heights that had never been witnessed before in the UK. He was the premier speed walker, and was a great ambassador for the sport. Lawrence Allen - my dad - was the man to beat, but not many did...until Roland Hardy. Over the following years, Roland and my dad were involved in many fantastic races, always with one sole aim in mind: to be the best! Winning was the ultimate prize; second was just not good enough.

Dad's passion took him to Commonwealth and European Championships, and the pinnacle in every athlete's career: the Olympic Games. Dad represented Great Britain at the Olympics in Helsinki 1952. Even now, after all these years and at the age of forty seven, I still find it painful to express the sadness I feel in what I believe my dad was cheated out of. Yes, an Olympic medal! If you read any sporting books which refer to the 1952 Helsinki Olympics, you will find much documented text on how badly the British race walking team were treated when decisions were made on disqualification of the whole British team. Much controversy surrounded those games with regard to the British. So very, very sad...

As dad will always say when I talk to him about those Olympics, 'It knocked the stuffing out of me. I won a few more Nationals after, but I was never the same race walker.'

Dad, in all his ninety-three years, has never managed to overcome the heartache of Helsinki.

My passion started at a young age. My sister Denise hanging on to my donkey on Blackpool Beach

Walking In Dad's Footsteps

'Pretty in pink' three bridesmaids. My sisters Sylv, Denise and me in the middle

Sport was always the main topic of conversation in our household, much to the dismay of my eldest sister Sylvia whom we usually referred to as Sylv. Sylv was eight years my senior and was quite motherly towards me on occasions, although sometimes I seemed to have the knack of irritating her with my childish antics, and she used to yell at me to desist. Sylv was always the typical young lady: pretty, very photogenic with cheeky dimples and a mass of dark hair as well as a lovely singing voice. Sylv, Denise and I attended our local church, and every Sunday morning we went to Sunday school, but it was Sylv who went on to be May Queen one year. Although I was only young I can remember Sylv, and her chosen Sunday School Captain, proudly walking around the congregation and up onto the stage to the sound of the New Seekers' 'The Carnival is Over'. She was crowned Queen Primrose.

Denise on the other hand enjoyed athletics and was quite a decent runner; but from a young age it was her back that became her Achilles heel. At the tender age of seventeen she had her first prolapsed disc. Mum and dad engaged the expertise of a specialist consultant who visited Denise at home; but it took weeks before she was able to get out of bed. I can remember vividly the nights I slept on a camp bed at the side of the single bed Denise was sleeping in. I used to try and console her by tickling her arm until the pain subsided and she could drift off to sleep for maybe an hour or two at a time. I never left her bedside until she could sleep through the night. Denise was sixteen when she started work at Sheffield University along with Sylv, who had also worked there since leaving school. Denise used to spoil me rotten in those days. Every monthly pay check she received she would buy me a present, or give me some spending money, or take me to town for me to choose something nice to wear. She was my soul mate as well as my sister. Denise and dad were my number one supporters throughout the time I spent in competitive athletics; they followed me just about everywhere around the UK to watch me compete. I represented Sheffield and Yorkshire on numerous occasions running 400, 800 and 1500 metres during the track season, and cross country during the winter. I suppose it's fair to say that I was blessed with a great deal of natural ability. I didn't really have to try that hard to achieve; it just came naturally and I did have a fair amount of success.

Unfortunately, the success that I was having in my athletics was by no means replicated in the classroom. After leaving Morley Street Junior School, later renamed Rivelin Middle School, I moved further away from my home on Manvers Road to attend Myers Grove Comprehensive School. Both my sisters had made the same transition, and now it was my turn. Academia was never really important to me at that stage in my life. Most of the time I spent daydreaming about the possibility of one day winning an Olympic Gold medal; how it would feel to be stood on the rostrum with the medal being hung around my neck; how I would turn toward the Union Jack to see it being raised aloft with the sound of our national anthem belting out across the Olympic stadium. Oh, how wonderful that would be! 'Elaine Allen, are you taking part in this history lesson, or would you like to tell us where you are? No doubt thinking about your next race!'

Most of the teachers were well aware of my athletic exploits, because most weeks I would be called onto the stage from assembly to be congratulated by the headmaster, or to be presented with a prize I had won the previous weekend. They say hindsight is a great thing; no one can turn the clock back, but how I wish I had paid more attention in the classroom and not wasted my school years. The sad thing is, I now know that I didn't do myself justice in my exams. I've proved that time and time again since. I only achieved mediocre CSE grades, whereas instead I could have achieved much more. By now I was sixteen, and very soon I would be leaving Myers Grove for good, to stretch my wings in the big wide world. There was no way I had any ambition or intention to stay on into the sixth form, so I needed to start looking for a job. Looking back I can't believe what a casual attitude I had towards a working career.

During this time in my life I was still being coached by the Sherwoods. Debbie was a good friend of the Sherwoods, and also a member of the squad. Although I was five years her junior, we did get along very well. We had known each other for some years so, when Deb knew I was looking for a job, she suggested I consider applying to the Sheffield Magistrates Court, where they were advertising a vacancy for a member of staff in the fines and fees department. I was fortunate enough to be accepted for an interview, and later that same evening I had a phone call from Deb. I was amazed when she told me that if I could 'keep it under my hat', the powers that be had informed her that I was going to be offered the job. Sure enough, five days later I received a formal letter offering me the position.

My time as a school girl was nearing an end and, to be honest, it couldn't come quickly enough. It had not been something I had embraced with open arms. Even to this day I have never really understood when people say, 'School days were the best days of my life.' They certainly were not for me.

However, I was now seventeen and, a couple of years prior to this, Sheffield had introduced the ladies 'Star Walk'. This was a nine mile course, three miles shorter than the men's race, and it was to take place on the same day as the men's, and around the majority of the same course. Again as was tradition, the day being Bank Holiday Tuesday in May, I decided I wanted a crack at it. Wouldn't it be fantastic to follow in dad's footsteps, especially if I could win it!

This wasn't going to be that easy. I needed dad's blessing and, after the trauma of Helsinki, dad had always been adamant that if ever a ladies' race walking was introduced to the sport, he certainly did not want me to be tempted to go down that route. 'It's not a free sport,' he would say, 'too many restrictions which aren't judged fairly.' I needed dad's blessing, and I wanted him to coach me.

It was a cold, wet January evening and, after much debate, dad had finally agreed to take me out for a training spin around our local area. 'Come on then, lets see how you walk; if you don't roll ya feet smoothly, you'll be no good, an' I'll tell ya,' he said. 'Okay, okay,' I said, 'give me a chance.' As we walked down Manvers Road I looked up towards the sky, where small snowflakes were starting to fall. They were sticking to my pale blue bobble hat, and I can remember turning to dad and saying, 'What a night to start training for the Star Walk.' He turned towards me and replied, 'Let's see what ya like first.' About 10 minutes into my initiation test, I was aware that dad kept dropping back now and again. I guessed that he wanted to see what my race walking style looked like, as the next minute he would be back at my side. This went on for the whole time we were out. Turning back into Manvers Road dad said, 'Pick up the pace and finish fast,' so that's what I did. From a sporting angle, dad has never been one to give out compliments willy nilly if they haven't been earned, so when dad said, 'Aye, yer not bad, yer place yer feet well… yer might make something,' I took that as an overwhelming vote of confidence. Yep, Star Walk here we come, I'd got dad's blessing. Two weeks into training, dad thought it would be a good idea to introduce me to the Sheffield United Walking Club. Dad had been awarded life membership after his sporting achievements, and was always a popular figure with them. The following few months was a gradual learning curve on the finer points of Race Walking. Dad planned a training schedule for me, building the training sessions up until I was physically strong enough to cope with them. He was very aware that, although I was seventeen, I was still a young girl, and he didn't want to stress young bones that were still growing. Maturity comes with gradual progression, and during dad's sporting life he had seen many promising young athletes pushed too hard, too soon and completely burnt out. He wasn't going to let that happen to me!

During the build-up to the race the club were of enormous help and support to me. I trained with them a couple of times a week to start with, and slowly I was beginning to reel in athletes who at first used to leave me for dead. The training was paying off and I was improving with every week that passed by. Derek Slinn was another coach for the club. He'd known dad for years, and he encouraged me train with his squad. This would enable me to have the additional help of other team members to improve my competition and speed. It was at this point I became friendly with a girl called Diane Wood. Diane was also coached by Derek, and over the following months and years we became firm friends. The first of June (competition day) was rapidly approaching, and three weeks before the race dad and Derek decided that it would be a good idea for me to walk the course as if I was racing it. Although I trained on the course at various stages of my build up, I'd never actually covered the whole distance; so Derek would be in charge of the stopwatch during the time it would take me to cover the 9 mile course at racing speed.

Let's see what I could do!

It had been hard walking alone. Derek and dad had been following me in the car giving me encouragement along the way, and at various points dad had joined in with me as a tow to pace-make for me. It had been some time since dad could match my speed and, although that showed how quickly I was improving, I can remember missing the camaraderie of dad permanently being by my side. During this latest training session I completed the course two and a half minutes inside record time. I was ready. I was finally ready, and I was hungry for success!

The Race

Tuesday 1st June had arrived. So many times in my mind I had wondered what I would feel like on such a monumental day: not just for me, but equally for dad. It was a big occasion and I so badly wanted to deliver. All the family would be watching and supporting, but I tried to keep focusing on the job in hand. Dad suggested that I warm up by jogging down to the area where the race was to start. This way I could have some time to myself, and hopefully stay as calm as possible.

As I approached Hillsborough Park, I can remember thinking how uncomfortably warm the day was. Crikey, this was going to make things even more difficult. Everybody had the same conditions though, so I tried hard not to think about it. The race was due to start at 10.30am, but it was only 9.30am. Already the pavements were rapidly filling up with people who wanted to secure a decent viewing position for the men's race, which was due to come through first. I was a local girl, and now and then I would hear people shouting, 'Good luck, Elaine,' as I jogged past. Due to dad being very well known in Sheffield, I had created quite a bit of interest in the local newspaper, and the press had been eager to interview me as the daughter of an ex-Olympian.

Eventually we were called to the start line. It was called an all ladies race, so I was surprised to experience 'ladies' jostling for a decent position; but I had been taught well and stood my ground. 'Ladies, on your marks, get set,...' The starting gun fired and we were off. The first bend was upon us quickly, and I could remember dad telling me to get off quickly to secure a good position on the inside of the bend. I felt like a formula one driver trying to find the correct line to accelerate out of the apex of the turn.

Manoeuvre complete and I was out in front. As I rounded the bend I can vividly remember seeing members of my family cheering and clapping as they spotted me out in front. It was an awesome sight. I felt so emotional, so proud, but I had to concentrate on the task ahead. It wasn't going to be an easy one. Halifax Road was the first hill challenge and, so soon into the race, was going to be tough. I glanced ahead and I was amazed to see the pavements full of spectators. What encouragement they gave me that day. As I neared the top of Halifax Road I could see dad in the distance, with mum at his side. The heat of the blistering sun was really intense, and I was hoping that soon I would be in a shaded area, where I could settle down and take stock of my position. My mouth was so parched and dry that I was finding it difficult to swallow. Dad shouted, 'Well done, lass. Try and relax on the downhill stretch. You're looking good. Just try and keep the rhythm. Don't push it for the record today. It's too hot.' I remember thinking, 'Bloody hell, this is hard work. I must be mad.'

I was settling into a new stride downhill, which was a welcome relief after the shorter uphill stride. Just a change of pace felt good as I tried to prepare myself for what was still to come. I was soon beginning to pick off some of the back markers of the men's race, which had gone through earlier. Dad had given me information about the leading men, and who was out in front. I wasn't surprised to hear it was the favourite, but he wasn't having it all his own way; the leading bunch was giving him a hard time. I remember thinking, 'Thank god I haven't got company.' Four miles in, and I was grateful for a comfortable lead. Blimey, the heat was making things so much harder than I had anticipated, and I was feeling desperately tired. Whether it was a combination of the occasion, the emotion and the heat I don't know, but I do know I wanted to get to the end. Dad, bless him, was always around the next corner, giving me words of encouragement, which was so comforting. It's funny, but I can still remember the colour of the shirt that dad was wearing that day; it was white with a blue stripe where the buttons fastened. Mum wore a short sleeved dress, which was pale blue, cream and white. How odd it is that I can vividly remember those things like it was yesterday. The human brain is so amazing yet, as I now know, so very fragile.

The remaining few miles seemed to take forever. The last big hill was Barnsley Road. I'd nicknamed Barnsley Road the 'Big Dipper' because that's just what it looked like as you approached it. Down the steep descent with a small dip in the bottom then up the steep ascent. Nearing the top I felt my legs starting to wobble uncontrollably. At first I couldn't understand what was happening. I was finding it increasingly difficult to keep a nice smooth roll to my walking style. For about twenty seconds I had to revert to walking like anybody else would. My style just broke down, so I just tried to focus on putting one foot in front of the other. I didn't realise at the time, but a spectator who knew me had got a message to dad to say that I wasn't looking too well, and that I could be in trouble. I honestly can't remember much about the following mile or so of the race. I was just concentrating on keeping moving. At times I was aware of dad jogging at the side of me, and hearing him saying, 'Elaine, Elaine, keep shaking your head. Try and follow the white line in the middle of the road. You've not far to go, lass. Just hang on. You're nearly there. You've got a big lead. Nobody's anywhere near you.'

They say hindsight is a wonderful thing, but on this occasion I'm not so sure it would have been. Little did I know that I had started suffering the effects of heat exhaustion and dehydration. In the men's race, that had already finished, the leading man had experienced what was happening to me, but unfortunately he had collapsed just one mile before the finish, and had been taken away in an ambulance to hospital for treatment. It seems bizarre to say but, back in those days, it was against the rules to take on water to drink in any race less than twelve miles. How things have changed… and for the better! That last mile, dad was with me every step of the way. As I approached Hillsborough Park, I could see the stadium in the distance. I could hear the cheering crowds, and I so desperately wanted to be at the finish line. My hair was plastered to my head with sweat, and my white vest top felt like it had been attached to me with glue. It was so bloody hot! The course record, which I so wanted to break, was now long gone, but it didn't matter. I had nearly achieved my goal. Entering the stadium was a feeling that I will never ever forget as long as I live. I felt like a superstar. The stands were packed full of spectators. So many people who knew me were shouting out my name and waving their arms around, clapping and whistling. As I stepped onto the cinder track for my final lap, I glanced over my right shoulder to where the finish line was. Dad had entered the stadium just behind me and, as I stepped onto the track, he shouted, 'Go on, lass, you've done it. You're on your own now.'

It would have been lovely to have dad crossing the finish line with me, just to enjoy the moment with him. But I know that for dad the win meant just as much to him as it did to me. I know that on that day, 1st June 1982, Lol Allen was a very, very proud man, and for me, well…I'd won it for Dad and that's all that mattered!

The Waiting Room

Over the past few years, the interior of the consulting suite at Thornbury Hospital had become so very familiar. The water dispenser still stood in the same place, as did the reception desk; even the décor was still the same, albeit except for a lick of paint. In 1993, following two years of chronic back pain, I'd had a laminectomy (disc removal from the back), then three weeks on traction and six months in a plastic jacket. Following the surgery I had around three years of day surgery, starting out at six week intervals, extending to intervals of several months; and here I was again with something new!

Had I done something really bad in a former life?

Oh, well, here we go again!

The previous week we'd had our first consultation with Mr Andrew Shorthouse, a general surgeon. He said he wasn't unduly worried when he examined me but, just as a precaution, he was going to take a needle biopsy. 'Most lumps of this nature usually disappear over a period of a week. It could even be a little cyst of some sort. Let's give it a week and see what happens; in the meantime we'll get you an appointment for a mammogram next week, and we'll take another look next Monday'.

Nigel and myself left his office and, as we approached the lifts, Nigel turned towards me and stated, 'Well, that all sounds reassuring doesn't it? I feel better about that now, don't you?' 'Yeah,' I answered. 'What's wrong?' Nigel said, 'You should feel pleased.'

'Hmm,' I thought, 'then why don't I?' I just had this awful niggling feeling in my gut that it was going to be bad news, even after the positive feedback from Mr Shorthouse. I still felt I was in deep trouble; call it a woman's intuition, but I just didn't feel convinced.

6.45pm: still waiting, Mr Shorthouse was running 30 minutes late. 'Great, just our luck,' I whispered in Nigel's ear, trying to be discreet. Nigel was looking more anxious than me, I thought. He was dressed smartly in a dark grey suit and tie, having been at work all day. I was wearing a pair of grey slacks and a black blazer with the Olympic brooch, that dad had given me, pinned onto the left lapel. It somehow gave me support in a strange way. Nigel was beginning to make me dizzy; he was up and down so many times to the water dispenser that he'd virtually drunk it dry.

The consultation suite was packed full of patients waiting to see their consultants, and I couldn't help people-watching and trying to decide what might be wrong with them. Was there anyone else in this room that had found a breast lump? The funny thing was that nearly everybody looked perfectly healthy, but who would know if they might be walking round with some horrible disease that lay undetected? We were sitting next to the reception desk, so we were within earshot of most conversations that were taking place. Eventually, a nurse came through the double doors and said to the lady on reception, 'Is Mr Sharp with Mrs Sharp?' We'd both witnessed the comment, but said nothing apart from turning towards each other with a knowing look. I shrugged my shoulders and smiled as Nigel squeezed my hand. Surely we would be put out of our misery soon, I thought. I just wanted to know what was going on.

Another lady appeared, whom I'd not seen that evening; 'Mrs Elaine Sharp?' she asked, as she held the door open with one hand. Nigel jumped up and took the door-holding duty off the friendly, plump lady, who proceeded down a corridor into a room on the left. I felt like I was on autopilot, as the grey-haired man stood up from behind his desk and held out his hand to me. I shook his hand and sat down facing him. Nigel did the same. The same familiar grey desk stood in front of us, with Mr Shorthouse behind it opening up a file, which I presumed had something to do with me.

'Well,' said Mr Shorthouse, 'the mammogram was clear.'

Nigel and I turned to face each other, but said nothing.

'But,' said Mr Shorthouse, 'the needle biopsy showed up a bunch of suspicious cells.' Like clockwork, we again turned to look at each other. The sound of Andrew Shorthouse' voice was resonating in my head, until the silence was broken by Nigel.

'Suspicious cells,' uttered Nigel. 'What exactly does that mean?' looking at Mr Shorthouse.

'Well, it doesn't necessarily mean that it's cancer. The lab report still states that it is probably benign, but I will need you back in tomorrow to remove the lump, to see what we are dealing with.'

By now I was oblivious to the words that were coming out of my consultant's mouth. It was almost as though the volume had been turned down, but the conversation was still going on.

Nigel, as usual, was bombarding Mr Shorthouse with questions, which he promptly answered as best he could, with fairly brief and limited information.

'If it is cancer, how do we need to deal with this? What will the treatment be? Will she need further surgery? Chemotherapy: will she need that? What if it's spread?'

Nigel was doing what he does best; like most engineers he looks at everything from first principles, gathering as much information as possible before he finds the best way forward; only this time he was out of his depth, and out of his comfort zone.

Mr Shorthouse did his best to reassure us both. 'Look, let's not pre-empt problems before we know exactly what are are dealing with.' He reinforced, 'I realise that this is a worry, but we need to remove the lump first, and then formulate where we go when we have firm results.'

Likened to zombies, we reversed the procedure that had taken place twenty minutes earlier. We stood up, shook hands, and the friendly, plump lady, whom we now knew as Brenda, showed us out of the office and back down the corridor.

'I'll be here to meet you tomorrow evening,' she smiled. Brenda put her arm around my shoulder and gave me a reassuring hug. 'It'll be okay,' she added.

I nodded, smiled, and turned to Nigel, who was doing his best to keep positive for me. The return journey back in the car seemed a long one, although in reality the distance was very short. Thinking back to that evening, my mind was so full of questions, but my brain couldn't articulate them in any sort of order to make sense. It was as though the playback button had got stuck in one place.

Surgery

Making visits to Thornbury hospital was becoming more of a ritual than I cared for.

We'd been back and forth so many times in the past two weeks, that I was beginning to think that the car would be able to drive itself there. As arranged, Brenda was there to meet us. 'Are we alright?' she asked, looking at us both. 'Yes, thanks: fine,' I answered, trying to sound very casual. Although now a hospital, the building is a very grand one, and not at all what you would imagine a hospital to be like. Thornbury was originally built between 1864 and 1865, when Frederick Mappin, the cutlery and steel magnate, commissioned architects to design him a new house. Mappin had previously been a master cutler in 1855 and went on to become Mayor of Sheffield in 1877/8, and a liberal MP in 1880. During World War Two, the house was used for storage by the Admiralty; until, in 1947 it was purchased by the newly formed NHS for £11,500, and subsequently used as an annexe for the Sheffield Children's Hospital.

A few feet into the entrance lobby is the reception desk, where you are first met by Thornbury staff, who try their very best to put you at ease. Immediately behind you is a very grand, mahogany staircase, which wouldn't look out of place on a film set. You could just imagine Lady Mary, from the cast of Downton Abbey, sweeping her way down the staircase into the arms of Cousin Matthew, and living happily ever after.

'You're on Mappin Ward. Do you want to walk, or take the lift?' Brenda questioned. 'It's on the first floor: not far to go'. 'Oh, we'll walk: no problem,' I answered.

Mappin Ward was familiar. I'd been on Mappin four years ago, when I was admitted for my laminectomy: room eleven, as I recall. As we followed Brenda up and onto the ward, I realised that some of the staff had familiar faces, and I wondered if some of them might remember me. Why would they, though? Right at the bottom of the corridor was my room for the overnight stay. We entered the room, which had my name printed on it and another sign saying, 'nil by mouth'. Ugh, I thought, that sounds familiar. (When you are admitted into hospital, and are due to have surgery the same day, you are unable to eat or drink anything because of the general anaesthetic. Hence the 'nil by mouth'.)

I was surprised at how large it was inside; it was more like a suite than a room. I didn't remember the other rooms being as large as this, previously. There was a two-seater settee to the left, which was covered in a denim-type material, with a matching chair just to the right of that. The bathroom was set back, and again I was surprised at how large it was. I can remember thinking that most hotel bedrooms would struggle to be as airy and nicely decorated as this. It was a shame that I might be a resident for sinister reasons. Nigel was unpacking my bag when a young nurse wearing glasses entered the room. It was difficult to guess her age; she was quite wiry, about my height (5'5"), and her hair was tied back neatly in a bun, with a white lacy head-dress on top. She reminded me of one of the kitchen maids from the 70's TV series 'Upstairs Downstairs'.

'Hello. Are you Elaine Sharp?' she asked, as she glanced down to look at the A4 sheet of paper she unfolded from her uniform pocket.

'Mmm, I am,' I answered.

'Well, I'm Claire, and I'm going to be looking after you while you're here,' she said.

'Okay, that's fine, thank you,' I replied.

By now it was about 5pm. We'd only been in the hospital for thirty minutes but it seemed much longer. We'd been told by Brenda that Mr Shorthouse would be in to see me before I was taken down to theatre, which would be around 7.30pm; so we had a few hours to pass before then. Nigel insisted that he was going to stay with me until I went down to theatre, although I tried to persuade him that I would be fine, and that I thought he ought to go to his mum and dad's for a bite to eat. I had a feeling it might be a long evening. 'Not a chance,' he exclaimed, and pushed the 'on' button on the TV remote handset. Countdown was on, with Richard Whiteley. It was quite a hit in the 90's. He was teamed with Carol Vorderman, the mathematical genius, who produced the consonants or vowels for the two contestants who were competing against each other. Nigel didn't care for it much. I enjoyed it, but I knew how much Nigel disliked Game Shows (and still does), so I didn't complain when he immediately changed channels. Nigel was looking more stressed than me, so I thought it better that he watched something that would distract him from the job in hand. Eventually the door opened and in walked Mr Shorthouse. By this time I had already been given my Nora Batty stockings to wear (anti-thrombosis), and my hospital gown; so I was laid on the bed, with Nigel sitting on a chair at the side of me. We did the usual pleasantries, and Mr Shorthouse asked if the anaesthetist had been in to see me, to explain what would happen when I got down to theatre. We told him he had, and that we understood what the procedure would be.

'Okay, any questions?' he asked.

I shook my head and turned to look at Nigel.

'How long will Elaine be in theatre?'

'Well, not too long,' answered Mr Shorthouse. 'Were you thinking of coming back tonight to see Elaine? Because, to be honest, she'll be very sleepy, and it's probably best if she rests as much as she can. I'm happy to ring you at home, though, to let you know how surgery goes'.

'Honestly, love, do that; I'll be fine,' I quickly added.

Decision made, Mr Shorthouse nodded to Nigel, then me, patted my leg, smiled, and said, 'See you in theatre.'

Shortly afterwards, the doors were opened by two members of the theatre staff (one man and one lady). Looking down at the folder he had in his hand he said, 'Elaine Sharp?' 'Yes, that's me,' I answered, as I shuffled off the bed towards the trolley that they had brought with them. 'Your carriage awaits,' he quipped. I hopped up and onto the trolley, where I was covered with a blanket, and reversed out of my room, and down the corridor towards the lifts to take me down to theatre. The theatre staff are lovely in Thornbury and try to put you at ease, making conversation about anything other than your impending surgery. Tonight was no exception.

Nigel, the two staff and me on the trolley squeezed into the lift, and descended down two floors. Nigel held my hand as I smiled to reassure him, but this was the end of the road for him. This is where he got off, but I had to go on. He squeezed my hand, leaned towards me, and gave me a gentle kiss. 'I love you,' he said quietly, looking into my eyes. 'I love you too,' I whispered, trying to keep a stiff upper lip. Then he was gone.

Diagnosis

The next thing I became aware of was opening my eyes onto a dimly lit room, where I could just make out an outline of a person stood next to my bedside.

'Hello, how are you feeling?' said a voice that I recognised as Mr Shorthouse.

My eyes felt heavy, and I struggled to get my mouth to work. 'I'm okay, thanks,' I burbled. 'Do we know anything yet?'

'No, not yet,' he answered. 'We need to wait for the lab results. It'll be a few days'.

The quietness was broken by the sound of the phone ringing on my bedside cabinet.

Mr Shorthouse picked up the phone, and to my surprise put the receiver to my ear.

'Hello,' I slurred.

'Hello, duck,' answered a surprised voice on the other end of the line, which I had now recognised as dad's, that is Nigel's dad; but ever since the day we were married I've always called Nigel's parents mum and dad.

'Ah, Dad,' I muttered.

Dad was obviously shocked to have been put through to my room, and clearly was disturbed by the sound of my seemingly drunken tone. 'See you tomorrow, duck, and love you forever.'

'Bye, Dad, love you'.

Mr Shorthouse took the phone from my ear, placed the receiver back on its hook, and I went back to the land of nod.

The following day was Wednesday 5th November, bonfire night, not that I'd be going to a bonfire. Neither was I bothered. I was told that I could have a light breakfast, which consisted of fruit juice and toast. The morning after night surgery usually results in light food, which was fine by me. I can't say that I had much of an appetite. My left boob felt quite sore. Naturally, I expected that, but I didn't expect to feel quite as groggy as I did. Mr Shorthouse had left instructions that I could be released mid morning, and that an appointment had been made for me to see him the following Monday evening, when I would be given the results. 'More waiting,' I thought, as I picked up the phone to ring Nigel. He wasn't going to like that any more than I did, but what could we do? We had no choice but to be patient, although I must admit that patience is not one of my virtues. I'm quite an impulsive person, and when I want something I want it yesterday. Nigel is a much more of a thinking person, and usually thinks things through methodically before he makes a decision, but very rarely does he change his mind once a decision has been made. However, I have been known to be able to persuade him to change his mind on occasions when it suits me! He's a big softy really when it comes to me!

Nigel came to collect me around elevenish, and straight away I could tell he was very agitated about something. Nigel has a very calm persona normally, but this morning was different. He was eager to know what Mr Shorthouse had said the previous evening; if anything had been said that morning. Had I seen Mr Shorthouse that morning? Why wouldn't we know any results before next Monday? Why weren't we going to get a phone call? I didn't know the answers, and I found Nigel's agitation starting to affect me. When we arrived home Nigel was like a cat on hot bricks. I'd never seen him so seemingly stressed before.

'I'm going to ring Mr. Shorthouse,' he sighed, pacing across the lounge.

'I just need to know what's going on. I can't stand this waiting. I just need to know what's happening,' he kept repeating.

By now I was feeling quite tense, my tummy was beginning to churn, and I had a headache coming on.

Nigel picked up the phone as I wandered in to the kitchen to put the kettle on. Why is it that everybody thinks a cup of tea will solve a problem?

'Hello, Mrs Shorthouse, Nigel Sharp speaking'.

By now I didn't want to hear any more. I switched on the TV and turned up the volume.

It turned out that Mrs Shorthouse had been quite sympathetic, and had promised to pass on the message to her husband, to explain our anxieties. She assured us that, if they had any results before the weekend, Mr Shorthouse would ring us with the news, whatever it was: good or bad.

Nigel explained that we were not the sort of people to fall into a heap, but we just needed to know: one way or the other. Placing the receiver back on the phone, he looked skyward and sighed. He looked totally drained. I put my arms around his waist, and held him tightly. He reciprocated, and wrapped his strong shoulders around my body. I closed my eyes and whispered quietly, 'I love you so much. Just hold me.'

Friday 7th November, 7.40pm

It was just something about Coronation Street. We'd decided to pop out for a Burger. In those days 'Yankees' in Sheffield produced fantastic home-made burgers, with a really delicious, gooey cheese sauce. We always asked for the burgers to be served on brown buns, with a side order of chilli and coleslaw and, of course, fries. We frequented the American Diner at least once a fortnight, due to the necessity for our burger/cheese fix. I wouldn't have exactly called it junk food, but I suppose neither would you call it healthy eating; but it didn't half get the taste buds salivating!

As Nigel grabbed the car keys from the key box next to the front door, I was hurriedly tying up the laces on my boots. Due to the renovation work still on going, I was sat on the small nursing chair, which was then situated in our dining room. This was open plan to the lounge, separated only by a six-tread staircase. Even now, sixteen years on, I can still vividly remember the sequence of events that took place immediately after. The phone rang, and for a few seconds neither of us moved from where we were. The TV was still on, and once again Coronation Street was nearing the commercial break. What was it with that programme anyway? The fast forward button must have kicked into action next, because I remember Nigel appearing from the hallway in a bit of a panic, up the staircase to the lounge, and picked up the phone. Normally, on answering the phone, he would repeat our telephone number. But tonight he didn't. Instead, he just said, 'Hello.'

'Oh, hello Mr Shorthouse,' he said, glancing down to the dining room, where I was still sat on the nursing chair. Silence followed for a few seconds. But it felt like an eternity.

'Okay, right, right, I see, okay'. I instantly knew something was very wrong. I continued to look at Nigel until he raised his head and pointed his thumb down, towards the floor. 'Oh, my God,' I said to myself, 'it's Cancer.' I had to support Nigel; this wasn't going to be easy on him. I stood up slowly, and walked up, and into the lounge. Nigel reached out for a pen to write something down, but his hand was shaking so much he was struggling to make sense of what he was writing. 'It's okay,' I muttered stroking his back. 'It's okay'. After several minutes he put the phone back on the hook, looking in my direction. He looked drained and ashen-faced. I had to say something but I couldn't think what, eventually blurting out, 'I know, I know. It's Cancer isn't it?'

His eyes looked sad and watery as he opened his arms and said, 'Oh, love!'

We held each other tightly, each with our own thoughts, struggling to make sense of what we had just been told. How on earth can I tell my mum and dad, I thought: Nigel's mum and dad: Denise: Sylv. In hindsight, I bitterly regret the way in which we broke the news to my parents. I rang them and told them via a phone conversation, which I regret to this day. We should have driven down to their home, and broken the news in person. After all, for a parent, I suppose you never envisage the possibility of losing a child in your own lifetime. What a bloody mess! Just to break the news and leave them with their own thoughts was bad, very bad. Dad is always the one on the surface who appears to cope, but inwardly I knew he would be hurting. Mum wears her heart much more on her sleeve, and so she was able to show her grief freely; although I know now that dad gave mum a pep talk, to tell her to try not to cry in front of me. I must say she did extremely well, most of the time.

Mr Shorthouse had explained to Nigel that I needed to have further surgery, because he couldn't be totally certain that he had got all the primary Cancer away. He wanted us to see him the following Monday evening, and the surgery would take place the day after: once again on a Tuesday. We were given the weekend to get our head around the situation, and then it would be back to business. Mrs Shorthouse was great through it all. She rang us on the Saturday, the day after we'd had the bad news, to see how we were coping, and I must say has continued to be of great support throughout my more recent health problems. We saw Mr and Mrs Shorthouse on the Monday evening (Tina Shorthouse is her husband's secretary). It was decided that, to do a belt and braces job, all the lymph glands underneath my left armpit should be taken. In medical terms 'a full clearance'. It's quite amazing just how quickly the human brain accepts the unacceptable in such a short space of time. It had only been 72 hours since we had been given the cancer diagnosis and here I was being so business like about the whole thing. I even made a joke of the fact that it had just taken so long to grow my hair and now I might lose it. 'Bloody marvellous,' I quipped, 'just my luck!'

Here we go again

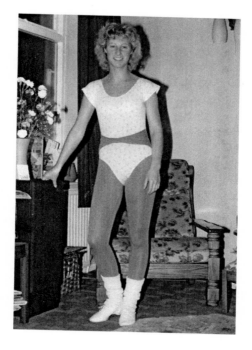

Nervously waiting to leave home for my first modern Jazz exam

The following twenty-four hours seemed to pass by in a bit of a daze. We acted out normal life on auto-pilot, trying not to contemplate what the outcome of the next lot of surgery might reveal. We had been told that it seemed likely that the breast lump was the primary cancer but, having said that, we were originally told that the lump 'didn't appear sinister', so we lacked confidence. We would just have to wait and see.

By now I was becoming familiar with the drill: the same ward (Mappin), the same nurses, the same theatre staff, all bar one or two, and of course Mr Shorthouse.

'We must stop meeting like this,' I said, smiling at Mr Shorthouse as he walked out from behind the theatre door. I was located in the little ante-room adjacent to the theatre, where heart probes were being attached to my chest. Mr Shorthouse was gowned up ready for business, and I felt a little bit like a lamb to the slaughter.

'Are we okay?' he said, squeezing my arm.

'Yes, I'm fine,' I replied. 'Is it Gin and Tonic time?' I grinned, as the anaesthetist tapped the back of my hand to try and find a vein to insert the cannula.

I know it probably sounds quite bizarre, but it's rather a relaxing feeling once the sedative starts taking effect: I would describe it as the 'Gin and Tonic' effect without the hangover. The sedative was taking its effect. Lying prostrate, the same faces I had been talking to earlier were now looking like something out of a comedy sketch: enlarged heads, rubber lips, bodies dancing like flames in a fire. Their voices became stuttered and distant. Taking a deep sigh, I decided to just accept my fate, close my eyes and disappear into another existence.

The peacefulness seemed very short.

'Elaine, Elaine, can you hear me?' a voice said.

I tried to open my eyes but they felt very heavy. I swallowed, and was surprised at how sore my throat was. It felt like somebody had been using an emery board on my tonsils (although I did have my tonsils removed when I was ten years old). My mouth was dry, and I really just wanted to be left alone.

'Okay, Elaine, have you any pain?' said the voice again.

I can remember thinking what a stupid question to ask somebody who had just had surgery; I was hardly going to feel full of beans!

Having said that, as usual I didn't want to sound like a wimp, so I answered 'No, I'm okay.'

My next recollection was waking up back in my room, where I had been just a few hours earlier. A night light was on and I could hear voices in the distance. My chest and armpit were hurting and, me being me, I just couldn't resist putting my hand underneath my gown to have a feel. 'Ouch!' Probably not a good idea, I was making matters worse. I was contemplating ringing my bell, when a familiar voice in a soft Geordie accent said, 'Now then, Elaine, how are you feeling, my love?' It was the ward sister, a lovely lady whom I was getting to know, 'Now, is there anything I can get for you?' she said, with a warm smile.

'Oh, I'd love a cup of tea, please, if that's okay?'

'Okay, I think you'll be okay to have one now,' she said, as she glanced at her watch, and back to my Ob's chart (observation chart where blood pressure, temperature etc. are recorded). 'I'll see what I can do.'

Ecstasy: the warm tea felt so good, and I savoured every mouthful. It was only 1.30am and, although I had some discomfort around my wound, the tea had been a welcome relief, and I did manage to doze on and off for the rest of the night.

The following morning, my first visitor of the day was Mr Shorthouse. It was only 8.00am, but the ward was already in full swing. Trolleys were being trundled up and down the corridors by nurses handing out pain killers, or by Thornbury staff serving breakfasts on neatly prepared trays. I was only allowed breakfast from the light diet menu because of the previous night's surgery, but I can't say I was bothered, as my stomach was churning somewhat, and I was already contemplating just having a drink.

Mr Shorthouse was keen to see how I was feeling. We talked through the op., and he told me he was happy with how the surgery had gone. He was fairly confident that he had been successful in removing all the diseased tissue, along with around 15/20 lymph nodes; the exact figure I cannot recall. Now all we had to wait for was the result of the lymph nodes: were they infected or not? Mr Shorthouse thought that they might be clear, but we would have to wait for the results from the lab. The lab results would prove quite significant on whether I would require chemotherapy or not. If the lymph nodes were clear then I would not, but if they were infected with cancer then chemotherapy would be essential.

How I hoped they would be clear! But it would be several days before we would know. The following few days seemed to be filled with twice-daily visits from Mr Shorthouse charting my recovery process, and a permanent influx of family and friends wishing me well. Although I had all the time in the world to rest, I felt completely shattered; and although family and friends meant well by keeping visiting times full, I was beginning to feel quite weary. I found myself glancing at the clock on the wall to see when I would be alone again. I guess, looking back, the fatigue was probably a combination of a number of different events. The shock of the diagnosis, several bouts of surgery, and once again waiting on results. In all, the length of time from discovering the lump to surgery was four weeks. I suppose it was beginning to take its toll, and it wasn't even over.

I can remember it was the Saturday evening, four days after surgery. It was around 6.00pm. Nigel was about to leave Thornbury to go to my mum and dad's for tea, before returning to see me for the evening, when Mr Shorthouse wandered into my room. I noticed instantly that his smile was not as bright as it had been over the previous few days. Nigel reached out to shake Mr Shorthouse's hand, and said 'Evening, Andrew, how are you?'

'Good, thank you,' he replied.

My evening meal had just arrived. I was sat up in bed, bolstered by an array of pillows. Knife and fork in hand, I was poised to tuck in to the delicious lamb roast that lay before me, when I realised that the paperwork Andrew held in his hand looked suspiciously like lab results.

'How are we today?' he questioned. 'Sorry: looks like bad timing,' as he glanced at my tea tray.

'Oh no, it's fine,' I said, smiling.

As usual, Nigel's quick thinking meant that he'd asked the service staff to keep my meal warm for me, before she exited my room. 'Of course: just give me a call when you're ready'.

Mr Shorthouse wandered around to the side of the bed where Nigel was stood, and waved the piece of paper towards us.

'I've got the lab results of the Lymph nodes. Unfortunately it's not what we'd expected but, having said that, it could be a lot worse'.

Again, the familiar feeling of déjà vu floated around my head. 'Here we go again,' I mused, as Nigel reached out for my hand.

The glands were infected, but only slightly. The prognosis looked fairly promising, so we had no choice but to get on and deal with the new situation we now found ourselves in. Chemotherapy was decided to be the best way forward, followed by 6 weeks of radiotherapy. It would be a belt and braces job but, if the outcome was successful, then so be it. Once again we had to try to be business-like; it was a means to an end, hopefully!

Somehow my roast lamb dinner no longer seemed appetising.

Nigel and Beyond

'Topping Out' Nigel and I open a bottle of Champagne on the ridge at Dobcroft Road. February 1988.

I was just 17 when Nigel walked into my life: he was 20, soon to be 21. I was very much a girl when we met but, unlike most boys I'd met, Nigel was not a boy, he was a man. He was tall, dark and handsome, and that's not a cliché, he really was. He was the double of my athletics hero Sebastian Coe. Needless to say, that was a massive attraction, the only difference being that Nigel was 6 foot 3 inches and chunkier. The very first time I laid eyes on him, I knew he was someone special. Over the following few months we became a couple but, more than anything, very good friends. We laughed a lot, and we were never short of subjects to discuss, which is quite amazing because Nigel was not the least bit interested in athletics, or any sport for that matter, apart from motor sport which he actively pursued. In fact, in his first road rally as driver, he took 3rd place in his Mark 1 Escort, and he was still on L-Plates! We took things slowly to begin with. There was no rush; we were young, and time was on our side.

Nigel's parents were both teachers: dad a headmaster and mum a primary school teacher. I can still remember, quite vividly, the panic which I felt when Nigel suggested that it was about time I met them. As a young, shy seventeen-year-old, it wasn't that long since I'd left school and, for some reason, I'd got this pre-conceived idea that meeting them would be similar to a pupil/teacher relationship. When I was at school, teachers were still very much held in high regard and well-respected. Sadly, today that is no longer the case. I couldn't have been more wrong. They were lovely, lovely people, warm and welcoming, and that has never changed. My dad always had a lot of respect for Nigel's dad and, after meeting them for the first time, my dad said 'He's a true gentleman.'

From the very early stages of Nigel and myself being together, I began to form a very solid relationship with both his mum and dad. Nigel was an only child and, as time went by, I very much felt like the daughter that they'd never had. Nigel's mum had had some complications throughout her pregnancy whilst carrying Nigel, and it was deemed fairly risky to become pregnant again; so, after much deliberation, they decided to be content with him.

From a very young age, Nigel has always been extremely sure and single minded about what he ultimately wanted to achieve in his life. I remember listening to stories from his mum and dad about when he was young. His practical talent for building and designing things was incredible, even at the age of eight years old. In a competition he entered at school, he made a model of a lighthouse. At the base of the lighthouse was a wooden wheel with four drawing pins in it. As you turned the wheel the drawing pins came past the wires, which made a connection, which in turn made the light flash inside the glass dome of the lighthouse.

This was made out of a potted meat jar; the lighthouse itself was made from a kitchen roll inner. The sad thing about this story is that he was disqualified from the competition, because the teachers/judges deemed the project to be too advanced for his years; therefore his parents must have completed the project for him!

However, for sometime Nigel had expressed his wish that one day he would build our home. Both of us were convinced that we would be together for ever, so looking for a building plot seemed the next natural progression. So, I set about trawling through what seemed like every Estate Agent in Sheffield for plots. Some were available, but were either too expensive for what we could afford, or in the wrong area. Nigel's mum and dad had always lived in the Ecclesall area and, after spending much time there, I had decided that this was the area in which I wanted to live. Nigel agreed, but there was just the small matter of money. Properties were expensive to buy outright, hence another good reason for building our own.

In early March 1986, I was just about to set off for work when the mail dropped through our letterbox. Judy, our little black and tan dog, had a nasty habit of attacking whatever came through the letterbox but, as luck would have it, this particular morning she was still upstairs snoozing on my bed. On hearing the clatter of the letterbox, I heard the familiar sound of paws jumping off my bed, followed by growls hurriedly approaching, as she scrambled downstairs for a letter breakfast!

'Ah, beat you to it this morning, Jude,' I laughed, as she slid to a halt on the vinyl kitchen floor. 'Better luck next time,' I smiled, as I bent down to give her a tickle underneath her chin. Defeated, she jumped back up the kitchen step, across the dining room carpet, and took a left turn: no doubt back up to my bed.

I flicked through the post I was holding, like shuffling a pack of cards, until I arrived at a brown envelope addressed to Miss E.H. Allen. 'Mmm, looks interesting,' I thought, as I turned it over to open. The letter was from the estate agents, advertising a building plot that was for sale on Dobcroft Road, Sheffield 11. I didn't know where Dobcroft Road was, but I realised that it was in the Ecclesall Area, because the postcode stated Sheffield

11. 'Oh, brilliant,' I thought. After ten months of unsuitable plots advertised, this one was just where we wanted, and it was up for sale at offers around £15,000. I wanted to ring Nigel straight away but, as I glanced up at the clock, I decided that I would be late for work if I did; so I would just have to contain myself for a short while longer until I got to work. Anyway, I knew that Nigel would be working by now, as he had an early morning run in his truck, to pick up 10 tonnes of limestone from one of the quarries for a customer. Mobile phones had not been invented in those days!

Several conversations later that morning with Nigel, we decided that we needed to act quickly, and have a look at the proposed building plot. First, I had to get the afternoon off work. Wednesdays were not one of the really busy days in the Fines & Fees Department, where I worked at the Court House, so it wasn't a problem asking for the afternoon off at short notice. Nigel has never been employed by anyone to this day; he's always worked for himself, so getting time off wasn't a problem for him. With living in the Ecclesall area all his life, Nigel knew exactly where Dobcroft Road was, but couldn't think where the plot could possibly be.

'Oh, I'm so exited Nigel, I hope this one's for us,' I said, as I jumped in the car beside him. Nigel always used to wait in the same spot whenever he picked me up from work. At the very top of Snig Hill in Sheffield town centre stood the South Yorkshire Police Headquarters. Adjacent to that stood the Sheffield Magistrates Court, which you approached via a steel and brick bridge. Invariably, I would run over the bridge and up the rest of the driveway towards where Nigel would park. This particular day I must have floated up there in blissful anticipation. On the drive over we chatted together about the prospect of finally finding a suitable plot for our first home together. Even Nigel was struggling to contain his excitement, which was out of character for him as he is usually very level-headed and calm in any given situation.

Eventually, we arrived at our destination. Nigel grabbed my hand as we strode over towards the 'For Sale' sign. We stood quietly together for a moment as though trying to absorb how the next decision might change our life for ever; it was quite surreal.

We turned towards each other and smiled, just a boy and a girl in quiet contemplation of what might be.

Six days later, I received the phone call that I'd been waiting for. It was a Tuesday afternoon, and I'd been on tenterhooks all day. Our first offer had been rejected, and today we had increased our bid; but this would have to be our last and final offer. A mutual friend of ours was a solicitor who specialised in conveyancing, and he was acting on our behalf.

'I've got it for you,' announced the soft voice on the other end of the phone. I paused, and then let out an almighty 'YEAH!' across the office. I was ecstatic, we'd got it, we'd got it! I couldn't believe it; I was so happy!

April 1986

After a few weeks of all the legal stuff being sorted out, we finally got the nod to say we were allowed to start work on our newly acquired plot. It felt odd that, after several weeks of just looking at the land, we were now the proud new owners of a small piece of land which, at this time, was still attached to Mr Fitzwilliam's garden.

Mr Fitz, as we called him, was an old chap who had been widowed for many year and, eventually, he had decided that his huge garden was of no use to him as just a garden any more. By selling off a portion as building land, he would be able to recoup some cash and still have more than enough garden for his own use. In fact, his remaining garden was larger than the plot we purchased! That gives you an idea of just how small our plot was. It was ours though: Nigel's and mine. It was the first time we had ever been joint owners of anything together, and it felt fantastic. In the previous weeks we had made Mr Fitz's acquaintance. We'd sat in his very large, but dated, kitchen, at the side of the Aga, on a window seat where we spent many an hour getting to know him. As it turned out, we became great friends over the coming months and years, and I do believe that he became as very fond of us as we did of him.

The day finally came when we could start work. It was a Saturday morning. We unloaded the car: full of shovels, picks, buckets and loads of enthusiasm. Nigel hopped over the small wall, whilst I handed the tools to him, and then jumped over beside him. It felt really strange; we almost felt like we were trespassing on somebody else's property.

I can still clearly remember the black and red jumper that I was wearing that day; Nigel was in his overalls. He'd ordered a pair for me, but they didn't stock ladies extra small overalls, so they were on special order!

We wandered the length and breadth of our plot, just familiarising ourselves with what we had to demolish, before starting the real building work. There was a small gazebo (greenhouse) with a few remaining panes of glass still intact. Loads of brambles and shrubs, which over the years had just run riot, blackberry bushes, old bricks (which had probably once been put there for the children to play build with); it was a mess and needed a good sorting.

I remember my mind feeling boggled at the work we had in front of us; only now did the reality of the mammoth task ahead hit home.

'Crikey, Nigel, there's so much to do. Where do we start?' I gasped.

Nigel, as calm as ever, just turned to look at me and said, 'How about here?' as he stuck his spade into soil surrounding a massive tree root.

So here it was!!!

It was certainly a day to remember, in more ways than one, I suppose you could say. This day I had a marriage proposal in a very typical Nigel way.

After the euphoria of removing the troublesome tree roots, and a very fruitful day's work, we started to load the tools into the back of the car, when Nigel said to me, 'Well, actually, I suppose we need to think about getting married.'

How romantic, I thought!!!

Married Bliss?

Finally we are married on 18th June 1988. A very happy day!

After being together for seven-and-a-half years, and being at the age of twenty-four years, my day did come at last.

On 18th June 1988 we were married, on a beautiful warm, sunny day, in St Oswald's church on Bannerdale Road. I was now Mrs Sharp, and it felt fantastic! It was what all brides dream of on their big day: perfect. The reception took place at Baldwin's Omega and, as we were driven to our venue in the open top vintage Rolls Royce, people waved to us, shouting congratulations. It was our local Ecclesall garden party, and the pavements were full of people leaving the event. The traffic was slow, which meant that we could enjoy the moment, and soak up the atmosphere of the day.

The first night was in our marital home, which was 154a Dobcroft Road, Ecclesall, Sheffield. After two years of building our home, it felt quite surreal to be carried over the threshold in my wedding dress, veil draped over my arm. 'Well, here goes then, stairs next,' said Nigel, taking in a deep breath. It's not that I was a heavy weight back then; in fact I only weighed 8stone 2lb, but the house was open plan. So much so, that in the rush to move in for our wedding night, we had not had the time to secure the handrail. The higher we climbed up to our bedroom, the longer the drop would have been if Nigel had lost his footing. After all, everybody has a few drinks on their wedding day, and so probably not quite as compos mentis as one would normally be, Nigel and I being no exception. Once outside our bedroom door, we'd made it safely...or so we thought!

'The door's jammed!' I exclaimed turning to Nigel.

'What? Can't be!' said Nigel, as he put his hand around the brass door knob, and pushed his shoulder against the door. Nigel's weight forced open the door to the sound of bangs and loud consecutive pops. What on earth was happening?...

Then, all was revealed. Our bedroom had obviously been hijacked! It was crammed full of different coloured balloons, that Nigel was inadvertently popping as he fell into the bedroom. At first we were stunned, and I just stared at the mass of balloons that engulfed Nigel as he grovelled around on the blue carpet that had been fitted only four days previously. As Nigel struggled to compose himself, I began to see the funny side of our little ordeal, and burst into hysterical laughter. Here was I, in my posh wedding dress, diamante headdress and 10ft veil, watching my husband of 11 hours rolling around on a sea of coloured balloons in top hat and tails..., how bizarre was that?

Either an individual, or a number of people were intent on making our wedding night a night to remember, and we had our suspicions! It was courtesy of MARK & SUE: thanks, folks!

Day one of married life started off as eventful as the previous evening. We'd spent all the money we'd accumulated on building our love nest, so had very little spare cash to go away on a honeymoon, let alone to somewhere exotic, like couples manage to do today. After all the hard work we'd endured building our house, Nigel was adamant that we went away for a few days for a little peace and relaxation. Both of us loved North Wales, which we had visited several times throughout our time together. A few weeks before we were due to marry, Nigel informed me that he had made a booking reservation for our honeymoon. It was for a four-night stay at an idyllic location, the 'Tyne Cornel Hotel', overlooking Tally Lynches Lake.

It was really strange, waking up in our new home the morning after our wedding day. It had taken us two years of hard graft to get here, but we'd finally made it. Yesterday morning I was Miss Elaine Allen, and today I was Mrs Elaine Sharp. This was going to take some getting used to. To start the day I decided that a relaxing, hot bath was just what I needed. However, it didn't quite turn out as planned. The run up to our wedding day, like most weddings, had been fraught. Trying to complete the house to a reasonable standard to move in prevented us having the time to flush through the plumbing system for a test run. Great! No matter how much water I ran, I never managed to maintain a clean run of fresh water. 'I think it's cleared,' I shouted to Nigel, who was still prostrate in bed. 'Oh, good,' he laughed, 'I'll jump in after you then.' No such luck: just when I thought it was safe to get into the water, the tap coughed and spluttered out another dollop of green flux! 'Oh, well, there's a first time for everything, I thought, and climbed into the bath anyway.

One hour later, to our surprise, Mark and Sue arrived with a bottle of Champagne and orange juice. It was a beautiful, warm, sunny morning, and the bucks fizz went down a treat.

When we arrived at the hotel, it was still as good as we'd remembered. A great addition to the facilities was a swimming pool that had just been completed. The weather was as good in Wales as when we had left home a few hours earlier, so we made the most of the welcoming, cool pool, and both had a quick dip before getting showered for dinner. Wow, married life seemed pretty good! Wales is very well known for having a great deal of cold, wet weather, but it seems the gods must having been watching over us, because we were blessed with blue skies for the whole of our stay. In fact, the weather was so good that we decided to delay our departure and stay at the hotel until late afternoon, so we could soak up the sun for a few more hours. Big mistake! Driving home that evening, Nigel looked decidedly ill, he was turning a lighter shade of pale by the minute. It could only mean one thing: sunstroke! Five days of marriage, and my wedding vows were about to swing in to action… 'In sickness and in health'.

Although Nigel and I were very much in love with each other, neither of us found the transition to marriage very easy. We had both lived at home up until getting married (although I did spend many nights staying at Nigel's mum and dad's) so, unlike many other couples of our age, we had never lived together. Nigel's mum used to smile and say, 'You know you're out of vogue not living together first.'

Yes we were, and that's just the way I wanted it. Not that I'm a prude or anything, but the idea of living together before marriage never really appealed to me, nor Nigel, for that matter. When one leaves one's family home, it's a massive adjustment to make, and both Nigel and I had a very warm, loving relationship with both our parents. It was tough, and I don't mind admitting that we had our fair share of arguments. Both of us would test the other, to see just how far we could push one another, before the other one would snap. I can remember, in particular, our first Christmas, six months into married life. Our mums and dads, along with Nigel's only aunty, were spending Christmas Day with us. I was cooking my first Christmas dinner, and I felt slightly nervous. Both of us were working full time, and as such we'd worked right up until Christmas Eve lunchtime.

I decided that I would prepare as much as possible that evening, so I wouldn't be left with so much to do on Christmas Day; then I could enjoy the festivities along with everyone else. As with some best laid plans, they don't always go as intended, and this evening was no exception. I became stressed about something as ridiculous as mince pies! I had been making mince pies for years. Why now were my pastry making skills deserting me? Well, for whatever reason, they were. Every time I tried to roll out the pastry, it just kept breaking up. Every time it happened, I got more and more frustrated. After mixing up five separate lots of different pastry, I was beginning to tear my hair out. By the time I'd done, I looked like an irate flour grader, and the kitchen looked like I'd whitewashed the walls with flour! Poor Nigel: I'm afraid he drew the short straw, and ended up with the wrath of my temper. By trying to offer me his advice, I took my anger out on him. Eventually, he got cross and I stormed upstairs in tears and locked myself in the bathroom.

Ooops, first rule of marriage... quit while you're ahead. Thirty seconds later Nigel was banging on the door asking why I was shouting at him. 'Elaine, this is stupid, they're mince pies for God's sake!' In desperation to reason with me, he banged on the door with such force that the bathroom door, complete with architrave, came falling in towards me. There was I, sat on the toilet seat crying when Nigel made his grand entrance. He was beginning to make a habit of falling in through doors, I thought. We were both so surprised at what had just taken place. Still sat on the throne, I glared at Nigel in silence. Nigel shook his head to regain his composure, and raised his eyes in my direction like a little, lost puppy. What a crazy scenario, we stared at each other and burst into laughter. Oh, bloody hell, now we'd got to repair the door! Fortunately, peace was restored, and Christmas Day went off without any hitches. A great day was had by all.

Boating and Juliet

'Juliet' Our first boat under construction in our front garden at Dobcroft Road

We had many happy years whilst living at 'Dobo', as we fondly used to call it. However, we also had difficult times. One month before were due to celebrate our first wedding anniversary, I found myself admitted into the infectious diseases ward at the old Lodge Moor Hospital. I've always struggled trying to keep weight on, so because of this Nigel has always encouraged me to eat food that will help me put weight on. Cream, off the top of the milk, was one of those and, although I don't like fatty meat or butter, I do like cream. So, every morning when we had our cereal, Nigel always sacrificed the cream off the top our milk so that I could have it. Unfortunately, we didn't take into account that when our milk bottle tops had been pecked at by the birds they were infecting it with campylobacter, and yes, you guessed, they were infecting me too!

It was really quite frightening at how quickly I deteriorated once the bug had got hold. Within a few days it had completely taken me off my feet, and my weight loss was dramatic. It took sometime for the lab to culture the bug; hence a two week stay in hospital, courtesy of Lodge Moor. Recovery was slow, which meant I had about six weeks off work before I was well enough to resume my normal 'day job'. The only good result was that Nigel had booked a surprise weekend away in Harrogate to celebrate our 1st wedding anniversary, which he presented me with a couple of days before. We had a fantastic weekend and still to this day go up to Harrogate to celebrate our wedding anniversary.

One year on, and we were settling in to married life very comfortably. We'd done the silly squabbles and heated arguments, testing how far we could push each other, and now married life was becoming married bliss.

Around this time I was eager to find a hobby that we could both share and enjoy together. Although I very rarely compete these days, at that time I still maintained my fitness with my first love, running. I was still running around 30 to 40 miles a week, which I found relaxing after a bad day at work. Sometimes I would come home, change out of my smart work clothes, put on my shorts, T-shirt and trainers, and just run for miles. It was my way of relaxing and feeling inner peace. Nigel, on the other hand, did not enjoy sport in general. Sorry: correction: he did enjoy motor sport, competing himself in his younger days, and was an avid follower of the World Rally Championship. Every November we would travel to North Yorkshire, or wherever the secret stages were being held, and follow the rally. Some were night stages, which were absolutely fantastic.

However, what sport/hobby could we do together? I had mused on this subject before, but never really came up with any inspiration until one day, whilst on my lunch hour, I was wandering around in W H Smith. I always looked at the magazines in the sports section, and often made a purchase, so I had something to read back in the office whilst nibbling on a sandwich. This particular day my gaze became fixed on a magazine called 'Practical Boat Owner'. As I thumbed through the pages I can remember thinking that this could be a sport/

hobby that we could participate in together: a joint interest. Yeah, this could really work! Nigel had owned a very small speed boat, along with a friend, when I first met him. In fact one year, at the age of 19, they towed the boat (named Skua) on the back of Nigel's RS 2000 to the South of France. I was becoming increasingly excited, when I glanced at my watch and realised that I had been flicking through the pages for the past 15 minutes, and if I didn't hurry up and buy the mag., I was going to be late back to work. Decision made, I hurriedly made my purchase. That afternoon I couldn't wait to finish work so that I could get home to talk to Nigel about my idea.

'Sailing: are you sure?' he smiled, as he looked down at the magazine. 'I didn't know you liked boats.'

'Well, I've never sailed before, so I don't know if I do, but there's only one why to find out,' I replied.

'How do you mean? What do you suggest?' he grinned.

With hands on hips, I grinned back and replied, 'Well, if you look in the index, there's a section advertising Sail Training Schools. Why don't we give them a ring, book on a week's course, and give it a go? There's a place called, "The Westerly Sea School." They look quite good.'

'Listen to you,' he laughed, 'someone's being doing their homework.'

Two days later I'd rung the sea school, organised a week off work, and booked the 5-day 'competent crew' course for two people. Bound for sea we were, in Milford Haven.

To pardon the pun I was hooked, line and sinker. Sailing was definitely for me. In fact I found I had quite a strong stomach for life on the ocean waves. If you've ever been sea-sick you'll know exactly what I mean! All we had to do now was find a boat to buy!

We had very limited resources, though, only one year into marriage. We had ploughed every ounce of cash into building 'Dobo', and had nothing left to spare. However, every cloud has a silver lining and, as luck would have it, one of ours did, in the form of a small investment I had being paying into since starting work. It was due to come to fruition, and what better use to put it to than investing in our very first boat? The boating bug had bitten and I was smitten, much to Nigel's delight.

Our search ended in the Lake District. She was a basic little sail boat (boats are always female, in case you didn't know), with a fair bit of work to do on her before she would be sea worthy, known in the trade as an 'unfinished project'; but she was all we could afford. We were not shy of work, and we were prepared to put in the hard graft to get her up to scratch before we could launch her. As Nigel's dad would say, 'You only get out of life what you put into it.' Crikey, did we work! Every spare minute we had, we spent working on her. Both of us wanted to get out on the water as soon as we could, and the only way to do that was by putting the work in. Every evening after work, every weekend: we were spurred on with the thought that we were nearing the day when she would be finished.

Several months later, and we were ready. We had secured a berth at Kingston-upon-Hull in the new Marina, in the King George dock. Watching the massive boat hoist lift her off the trailer and into the water is something I will never forget. All the emotions that had been building up throughout the past months were now able to flow out. It was a proud moment, and yet another sense of achievement for both of us. We'd completed her together. Nigel does not show his emotions outwardly and, like his mum, doesn't wear his heart on his sleeve, but what I will always remember is turning towards Nigel to see a very emotional man. Tears running down his face, as she was placed in the water. If that's not a sense of pride and achievement, I don't know what is!

'Juliet' was born! We named her 'Juliet' because, as two young people falling in love, 'our tune' was Dire Straits number one hit single 'Romeo and Juliet'.

Close to the Wind

'Ocean Breeze' our second boat arriving at Hull Marina prior to launch. I'm in the foreground looking on nervously

Too close on one occasion! 'Ocean Breeze' was our second boat. At 35ft she was a capable go-anywhere boat; many smaller yachts than her have circumnavigated the globe. She'd been built to a high standard and a top spec; we knew this because we had built her. I myself had laid up every sheet of fibreglass, saturating the cloth with a pre-mixed quantity of resin and catalyst. You had to work quickly, because you only had around twenty minutes before the resin would 'go off' and set rock hard. On the other hand you had to make sure your work was accurate and precise, because one day your life might depend upon it! Ironically, ours did!

If you've never stepped on, or inside, a sailing boat, then it's going to be difficult to explain, but I'll do my best. From a layman's point of view, nothing sounds logical on a boat. Externally, on deck, you have the bow, which is the front of the boat, with a safety rail around it known as the pulpit. The stern is at the back of the boat, with another safety rail, the pushpit, and the greatest width across the boat is known as the beam. Ropes which hoist sails are called sheets; other ropes are classed as lines, and others classed as warps. How are you doing? I know, it sounds crazy! I'll continue. 'Ocean Breeze' had two sails, a mainsail and a foresail. Sometimes, when sailing downwind, generally in light breezes, we could set a spinnaker (a huge extra sail) to push the boat forwards more quickly. The boom is what the mainsail is hoisted on, and when you want to go straight ahead against the wind, you need to 'tack', by taking a zig-zag path, first steering left (port) and then right (starboard), and to perform each turn you say 'ready about'. The steering position is the helm, which is in an area known as the cockpit. Internally, it's still as confusing. The seating area is called the saloon, the kitchen is the galley and the bathroom is classed as the heads; honestly, it's true! Up forward, is sometimes termed the 'fo'c'sle'. (This is from the yachting glossary, short for forecastle). Finally, the rear end of the boat is called 'aft'. If you can make sense of all that you've done extremely well.

Thinking back to that nearly fatal trip still gives me the shivers. It is one which I will never forget, as the fear I felt was so vivid! It all started on a beautiful August morning. We were then berthed in Kingston-upon-Hull Marina. We had planned a trip to Brancaster, which was situated on the north Norfolk coast. Our estimated passage would take around twelve hours, so it would be no mean feat for our first trip. From our marina we first had a twenty mile sail down the river to Spurn Point. Spurn Point is quite a landmark for sailors in that area. It's where the lifeboat station is located, and it is also the last safe anchorage before entering the North Sea. We had decided that it would be sensible to sail down the Humber estuary the night before, and anchor overnight. That way we could get started at dawn the next morning in order to make landfall in daylight. Once we had anchored we set to preparing supper, which consisted of beans on toast, washed down with a glass of milk. The sunset that night was fantastic. We sat on deck until darkness fell, then retreated down into our comfy berth (bed), and fell asleep dreaming of our adventure.

The following morning dawned, and with it was a hazy mist. We had expected this though, as it's quite usual at that time of year after prolonged hot weather. We were grateful, however, that it soon cleared. It can be quite daunting starting a passage in those conditions, and the last thing you need to be worrying about is the weather. In actual fact the skies cleared sufficiently, and the sea was so calm, that we had to motor part of the trip because of lack of wind. It was like being in the doldrums. I baked fresh bread for lunch, and we were soon tucking into salmon and cucumber sandwiches, which went down a treat: scrummy. Sixty miles of open sea, and we were nearly there. As we approached the harbour there were people on jet-skis, water skiers, lots of boats, and people enjoying the warm evening sunshine. It was great! Whilst Nigel carefully navigated Ocean Breeze through the myriad of people, I radioed through to the harbour master to inform him of our imminent arrival. We soon spotted the harbour patrol boat with him on board. Once within shouting distance of Ocean Breeze, he directed us to the mooring buoy we had been allocated for our three-night stay. Or so we thought.

We kept a small dinghy on the back of the boat and, after showering and getting dressed for the evening, we rowed ashore, tying the dinghy to a small wooden jetty. We strolled into the village chattering about the day's events. We both felt a real sense of achievement, and promised ourselves a lovely evening as a reward. The village was small, but there were quite a few pubs to choose from. We decided on one that had a good restaurant; after all, we were going to spoil ourselves tonight! The pub seemed very popular with the locals; the only downside to this was that they said there would be at least an hour's wait for a table in the restaurant. In truth it ended up being more like two. However, at the time, we wanted to have an hour in the bar to relax and have a drink or two, or three or four as it turned out. In hindsight, our mistakes that evening were a catalogue of errors. In our euphoria of having a successful passage, we had neglected to remember all the basics that we had been taught. Firstly, what state of tide would it be when we wanted to return that night? In essence, would we have any water to row back in the dinghy? As we approached the little wooden jetty in the pitch-black darkness we could see our dinghy, but it was now sat on the sand. In those days we didn't have mobile phones, so we had no means of seeing in the dark. That was the second mistake, we had forgotten to take a torch.

Thirdly, we had to wait so long to be seated in the restaurant that we had drunk too much, even before we started on the wine! I don't suppose the liqueurs helped either! Anyway, it's for all these reasons that we found ourselves in this predicament.

'Oh heck, bun, what shall we do now?' I gasped.

'Well, we need to retrieve the dinghy,' he replied.

'Off you go then,' I laughed, and 'I'll wait here.'

By now, our eyes were slowly adjusting to the darkness but, although I could just make out Nigel's outline, it was becoming increasingly difficult. The night air was still warm, but the breeze had taken on the familiar chill of the sea. Suddenly I heard Nigel's voice, 'Oh, bloody hell, no.' 'Nigel, Nigel, are you okay?' I shouted, slightly panicked by the tone of his voice. I could hear sloshing sounds, followed by spurious swear words, coming from the vicinity of where I guessed Nigel was. I was peering into the gloomy darkness trying to catch a glimpse of Nigel, when something caught my eye.

'Nigel, Nigel, is that you? Are you okay? Have you got the dinghy?' Sure enough, albeit a little dishevelled, Nigel finally appeared, staggering out of the darkness. 'Oh my god, bun, what's happened to you?' I said, trying not to laugh. 'What's happened to me? What's happened to me?' he replied. 'What's it look like? I'm up to my knees in bloody quicksand!'

The dinghy was nowhere to be seen! Nevertheless, I was relieved to see Nigel in one piece. Whether it was the relief of knowing he was safe I don't know, but I started laughing uncontrollably. There he stood, his cream chinos now looked more like two-tone trousers, and his pale blue shirt looked like a tie-dye design of mud, sea and sand. Fortunately, Nigel did see the funny side, and together we dropped to our knees laughing until our sides ached.

The initial frivolity over, reality hit home; we were then faced with the dilemma of how to get back on board Ocean Breeze. After thinking through various options, we decided there was only one sensible solution, and that was to head back to the restaurant. 'When all else fails, head back to the pub,' so that's what we did. By the time we returned to the pub it was quite late, and most of the customers were making their way home; only our home was high and dry, literally! Fortunately, the manageress was really helpful and, after we explained our predicament, she told me about a bed and breakfast that was about half a mile down the road. Our second lucky break was that she knew the proprietor, and offered to put a call through to see if there were any vacancies for a bed for the night. Hurrah! Maybe our luck was beginning to change - a room was available.

Now then, for some reason I've always had problems with left and right. So much so that, on my final driving lesson, an hour before my test, my driving instructor told me to take a right turn. I was confused. The only right turn imminently to my right was a petrol station. I glanced down at the fuel indicator, to see that we still had just over half a tank left. Surprised at the amount of fuel we still had left I continued to make the turn. Obviously, the instructor didn't like dropping below half a tank, I thought. Surely this was a trick question though? The instructor wanted to see that I was well aware of what my instrument dials were telling me? Smugly I pulled in at the side of the petrol filler and turned off the engine. Hmm, she wasn't going to catch me out! Wrong, wrong, wrong! When she glared across at me with a blank expression on her face, I realised my stupid mistake; I'd turned left instead of right - how embarrassing! Anyway, moving on swiftly, we'll get back to sailing!

Nigel had flatly refused to re-enter the pub with me because of the state of his attire, so it was down to me to organise a B&B for the night. Success! After securing a room, I listened to the directions of how we could find the B&B. It seemed fairly straightforward, even for me to understand. So, off we went. It wasn't until the alcohol started to wear off that I started to think we'd been walking a long time. Surely by now we'd covered the half a mile to our destination? The August night air had definitely taken on a chill. We were both getting tired. I was beginning to feel cold, and we both just wanted to climb into a comfortable bed. No such luck! The stinking mud on Nigel's legs had now dried to a hard crust. The only consolation to this was that the smell had disappeared, but the crustiness of the mud had started to cause blisters on his feet. He wasn't a happy bunny, but neither was I, and the evening's escapades no longer seemed amusing. It was Nigel who decided enough was enough. It was also pretty obvious that the colour of my hair had once again earned itself the well known saying 'dizzy blonde'. Yes, I'd messed up again. I was so cross with myself; could I ever get anything right? Eventually, we retraced our steps. Once again, I was in the pub for the third time that night; but this time Nigel was adamant he would be right behind me. Hallelujah!

After explaining what had happened, we were taken pity on. A member of staff was heading our way and offered to take us to the elusive B&B. On arrival the house was in darkness. Mind you, that wasn't surprising, because we were about two hours later than expected. What now? We had two options. We either spent the night outdoors, or somehow tried to wake up the occupants of the house. In this instance, discretion being the better part of valour, we plumped for the latter. We decided that we had to be discreet, so it seemed to me that we should go round to the back of the house, where we would at least be hidden from the other houses on the cul-de-sac. Aided and abetted by Julie (the staff member), we made our way around to the back garden. A dim light was still shining in one of the rooms: thank goodness! We presumed from this, that at least somebody was still awake. The three of us stood in the garden, like three naughty school children, looking up at the window. Nigel picked up a small pebble and tossed it upwards towards the window, swiftly followed with a whisper of 'Hello, hello.' After several attempts, we stood looking longingly towards the window, when noises were heard. The clinking of keys and locks were heard, and then a door opened.

'I'd given up on you,' said a voice from the door.

Nigel replied, 'I'm so sorry about this, but we've had a few problems trying to find you.' Then Julie spoke, 'Hello, Mary, this is the young couple from the pub.'

It was a starry night. The sky was full of stars that twinkled like diamonds. The garden was illuminated with a warm, yellow glow which, in a strange way, made the whole scenario seem more plausible. A brief explanation took place, and then Mary turned to Nigel, looked at his legs and asked, 'So, what happened to you?' Rather embarrassed, Nigel explained. I added the odd comment or two in-between, trying not to laugh. It was impossible though, and then a warm bucket of water, soap and a towel was handed to Nigel to clean himself up! And all whilst in the garden!

Relieved finally to crawl into a bed, we snuggled up together to take a well earned rest. Not surprisingly, sleep came easily that night.

Enjoying lunch with mum's and dad's onboard 'Ocean Breeze' our 2nd sailing boat

Mayday

On opening my eyes the following morning, my immediate thought was 'Where am I?' Rubbing my eyes, I recalled it was the morning after the night before. Crazy!

Nigel was beginning to stir at the side of me, and he turned to face me, whispering, 'Morning.' I kissed the end of his nose, and pulled back the covers to go to the bathroom. 'Oh my god, bun, look at the state of the sheets, they're black,' I cried.

With complete consternation, Nigel looked back at me and said, 'Well, how could I get totally clean in what was just a bucket of water?' I must admit, he did have a point. To evade further interrogation from Mary, we opted to skip breakfast and make a hasty retreat back to Ocean Breeze. It was a beautiful morning, and the garden that we had entered the previous evening took on a completely different feel in the warm sunshine. An abundance of colourful flowers was tucked into every nook and cranny. Pink cherry blossoms hung above the small gate, giving off a wonderful aroma. Honey bees were buzzing around busily collecting pollen and yeah, life felt good. Following Mary's precise directions, we soon had the harbour within sight. We'd overheard a conversation in the pub the night before. Forecasters were suggesting that a break in the weather was imminent. To be honest, the wine had been flowing rather well that night, so we dismissed the idea without much more thought. That was until now. The wind seemed to be strengthening somewhat, and I couldn't help but recall the conversation I'd heard several hours earlier. However, I tried to put that to that back of my mind, and think positive thoughts. Not that easy when you tend to be a pessimist!

When we reached the harbour jetty, it was comforting to see our little dinghy once again afloat. In no time at all we were clambering up the transom steps to board Ocean Breeze. It felt good to see our familiar surroundings and possessions on board again: our floating home comforts, as we often used to say. We were determined to make the most of our first full day's adventure. We shopped, chatted to locals, and even took a dip in the sea, before settling down with a cool beer in the cockpit. What a civilised way to spend a day.

During the night, I was awakened by the sound of masts clinking; the wind was definitely increasing. It occurred to me that it would be good seamanship if tomorrow we picked up a metfax from the harbour office, to take a closer look at the forecast. Snuggling back down in the quilt, I took a deep breath, and went back to the land of nod.

It wasn't looking good, I groaned, as the metfax gradually printed out. Low pressure was building from the northeast, which meant we would have northerly winds, as the wind blows anti-clockwise around low pressure.

We would definitely have to postpone our departure for home. It would neither be safe nor pleasant sailing in those conditions.

Four days later, and still the outlook didn't look great. We'd been obtaining a metfax daily to reassess the weather forecast. After much debate, Nigel suggested that he thought that we might have a small window of opportunity to sail the following day; it would be tight, but possible. In instances such as these I would always bow to Nigel's superior knowledge; if he thought we could do it, I trusted his judgement completely.

We prepared as best we could for an early departure the following day from Brancaster to Hull. Nigel made all the relevant engine checks, oil, fuel, coolant and fuel reserves, and all was in working order. I'd prepared cheese sandwiches the night before as, with such an early start the following morning, I didn't want the added bother of making sandwiches. I would have enough jobs to do.

When we turned into bed that night I wondered what tomorrow would bring. Calm seas and light winds would be welcome, but I knew that was not going to happen. Sleeping was difficult. We were both restless and we tossed and turned whilst listening to the wind blowing in the rigging. When I eventually did find sleep, I dreamed of the sail home. Phew, I was tired already!

We were both awake before the alarm clock started to ring. No doubt Nigel was as apprehensive as I was. However, we both kept our thoughts to ourselves, and got on with the job in hand. After pulling on our foul weather gear, we opened up the hatch, and stepped up to the cockpit. 'Flipping heck, Bun, the wind's blowing hard. It must be 25 knots'. Actually, when Nigel took the cover off the instruments, the wind speed was showing 32 knots! It didn't really fill me with confidence, seeing the look of shock on Nigel's face. He was usually so calm: but not today! Shielding his face with his hand, he turned towards me and said, 'We've just got to get home, love. I need to get back to work. We've been here ages, and we just need to get home.' So, with that, I resigned myself to the fact that we were going no matter what, and I would just have to get on with it. Nigel instructed me to clip my life line onto a jackstay, before heading up forward to slip the mooring lines attached to the buoy. I did so without hesitation, as I didn't fancy a man overboard drill today!

As we headed out into open water, I can remember feeling a sense of panic. If it was this bad now, here, what would it be like three miles offshore? I shuddered at the thought of it. Nigel asked me to take the helm, whilst he went up front to set the sail. In all our years of sailing we'd never had to set the storm jib before, but he did this day. This was another first, and one which unnerved me even more.

Two hours into our journey, and we were committed. Even if we had decided to turn back to safety, because the tide was going out we wouldn't have had sufficient depth of water to do so. No, we had no option but to continue onwards to the mouth of the Humber. Both of us were feeling ill. Nigel had taken some anti-seasickness tablets, as sometimes he had the tendency to be sick. Fortunately for me, I didn't really suffer from sea sickness… that was until today. I had never experienced such foul weather before this trip: and not since, either. The seas were huge. Green water hurtled down our side decks with such incredible force. Our fixed windscreen did little to shield us from the relentless pounding of the waves, and both of us found ourselves gripping onto anything we could get hold of, to prevent being thrown around the cockpit. 'Good God,' I thought, 'it's more like white water rafting than sailing.' Poor Nigel: he was being horrendously sick but, to make matters worse, the anti-seasickness tablets he'd taken had a side effect of making one drowsy. I was horrified to find him falling asleep. 'Please bun, Nigel,' I yelled, 'please stay awake. Please don't leave me on my own. Please, bun, I need you to stay awake.'

His answer was simply, 'I want to get off.' My reply was, simply, 'So do I, but we can't. We've just got to hang on, and get through this together.'

For the first time in my life, I can honestly say I feared for my life!

I had to do something constructive: something worthwhile. I took the decision to radio through to the coastguard. Channel sixteen is the emergency channel that you listen to whilst out at sea, and the channel you make contact on. I had to know if the weather was due to improve or worsen. We'd been listening in on sixteen so we were already aware that other yachts and boats were in trouble. Maybe the coastguard could advise us. The news was not what I was hoping for. The extreme conditions had caught everybody out. This had not been forecast, and it was freak weather. After going down below, I shakily plotted our position on the chart, so I could give the coastguard a latitude and longitude of our position. My hand hovered above the radio set, whilst I rehearsed over and over again what I was about to say. As I gripped the handset, another call was coming through on channel sixteen. A man's voice said, 'Mayday, mayday, mayday, this is fishing vessel Lady Rose, Lady Rose, Lady Rose. I have eight persons on board and I am taking water on board rapidly. My position is two nautical miles southwest of the Humber river.' A man's voice gave a lat and long and then he was gone. Without a moment's hesitation, I grabbed the handset and spoke. My thoughts were that, if a fishing boat was taking water on board and in trouble, what flipping chance did we have?

It transpired that several other yachts in our vicinity were also struggling. I'll never forget that one of the other stricken yachts was called 'Snowgoose'. The Coastguard's opinion was that all of us 'yachties' should head towards each other, so that we could travel towards our destination with the confidence and safety of each other's company. In essence that seemed a good idea, until I plotted their positions. They were some distance downwind of us, and the thought of turning back to join them didn't fill me with much enthusiasm. We'd fought hard to get this far. Neither of us relished the idea of losing the distance we had travelled. After a brief discussion with Nigel, we made the decision to plough on regardless and go it alone. We'd come this far and we were not about to give up now. With gritted teeth I made my way back up the companion way steps to the cockpit, just in time to throw up over Nigel's wellies! What the hell, the sea would wash them off! On one occasion we tried to eat some of the sandwiches that I'd made the night before. Old seamen will tell you that you should never go to sea on an empty stomach, but it was just impossible to keep any food down. After chewing the cheese sandwich until it was mulch I spat it out and gave it up as a bad idea.

Between the peaks and troughs of the swell, we could occasionally see the tops of the other yachts' masts. When we were on the crest of a wave, and they were in a trough, their masts were just visible for a second; then once again we would be flung down into the abyss, not knowing what fate may have in store. Many times I thought about the layers and layers of fibreglass matting I had so painstakingly applied onto Ocean Breeze's hull. My motto had always been, 'If in doubt, put another layer on,' and that's just what I did, every time, and boy was I relieved now! It's odd the sort of things you think about at times like these, but I can remember thinking that we'd never made a will, not that we had much money in those days, but I was saddened for our families that they would have the added stress and heartache of sorting out our small estate. I'd never really thought about death up until now, don't get me wrong. I wasn't terrified of dying, but neither was I inviting it. I can remember thinking that at least we would go together, but I hoped it would be quick!

The hours slipped by as we sat motionless in the cockpit, sitting opposite each other, with our feet on the cockpit seating. This was the safest position for bracing ourselves against the constant buffeting of the seas. Looking over the bow of the boat wasn't for the faint-hearted; it was terrifying. At least, opposite each other, we were facing the sides of the boat. Sitting out the storm was our only option. After what seemed like an eternity,

Nigel thought he'd spotted Spurn lighthouse. To confirm this though, we needed the binoculars that were hung up by the chart table opposite the galley. Out of the two of us, I perceived that I would be the likelier candidate to go down below and fetch them. With Nigel's track record, I just couldn't face clearing up all the sick downstairs as well upstairs and so, reluctantly, it would make sense for me to go. Nigel was correct; waiting for a lull in the wind I peered through the 'bins'. Thank God: Spurn lighthouse came into view. In fact, it was another hour and a half before we wearily entered the safety of Spurn Point. The lifeboat was still out on duty, no doubt rescuing some other poor souls.

Moving on

After eight happy years in our first marital home, that we had painstakingly built ourselves, we began to feel like it was time to spread our wings and move on to yet another building project. We had many fond and happy memories to take with us, but for some time now we had both felt the pull of the countryside. Both of us had fallen in love with the picturesque Mayfield Valley, which lay just five minutes up the road from where we then lived (Dobcroft Road). We wanted the freedom of the rolling countryside, yet still wanted to be within striking distance of the city below, and ultimately still be fairly close to where our parents lived. The search began in earnest, but just how long would it take us? Nine months to be exact. By Christmas 1995 the deal was signed and sealed. We'd done it: Bassett House, Bassett Lane, Mayfield Valley was to be our new address, and we were ecstatic! Just one little problem - well, quite a big problem as it turned out! The property required a very great deal of work and money spending on it to bring it back to its former glory. The work we could manage. It was the money that was lacking!

Bassett House dates back to the 16th century when, as a group of cottages, it was known as Far Bassett Houses. As the years went by the 'Far' was dropped and Bassett Houses became the workers' cottages (four in total), that served the nearby Yarncliffe House Farm.

In 1967 the cottages and land had been purchased by Mr & Mrs Brooksbank, a well known family of Sheffield cutlers. The four cottages were partially demolished, and then extended to create Bassett House. The new Bassett House was designed and constructed as a modern 1960's open plan house. In the summer of 1969 the new occupants took up residence in the newly named 'Bassett House'.

Wednesday 1st May 1996

So here we were again: familiar ground, another project, another chapter, only this time we had no comfortable parents home to go back to after a hard days work. We would have to live on a building site whilst we completed the refurbishment. We had left the comfort and cleanliness of our newly built home, and replaced it with a wreck of a home. We had expected it to be difficult, but even so I don't think we had anticipated just how difficult it would be, living in and refurbishing the property at the same time. The house was in a really bad state of repair. Nigel decided that, to do the job properly, we would have to take all the walls in the house back to bare plaster, and start off with newly plastered walls. At least that way we would have nice clean straight lines to build upon. The kitchen was the first room that we stripped out, demolished existing walls and rebuilt new ones. All the materials that had been used in the original rebuild in 1967 were proving to have been built very solidly, and so it was pretty hard going to progress the job at any sort of speed. The work was laborious and time consuming, but we were very fortunate that we had very good dads who worked alongside us, just like they had done when we built our first house ten years previously.

Although Nigel's dad was a headmaster and, as such was a professional teacher, he was also an excellent joiner. In his much younger days, dad had built all the furniture for their own home when mum and dad had become engaged to be married, and the furniture still performs the same tasks today as it is still in use. The four of us always worked well as a team so, as the project progressed, we allocated ourselves different tasks to work on, to see through to the end of completion. I've always been the type of person to take pride in a job, or in anything, for that matter, that is solely down to me. I don't really like relying on other people, because sometimes they can let you down. I guess that's why I was never very keen on team sports. I've always thought that if you are in total control of your own destiny, then you've only yourself to blame if it all goes wrong. Team sports are all about being a good team player and working together as a team, but I always found that I would get really frustrated if someone, say, dropped the baton in a relay race when we were in a strong position to win. Maybe that's where I get my competitive spirit from. My Dad is just the same though, so I suppose I get it from him. I can remember that as a child I was always a bad loser; I hated to lose at anything, regardless of it being sport, or even just a board game. I always wanted to win, and I suppose that's stayed with me throughout my life. If you're faced with a negative situation then you must always fight. Sometimes you are not given a choice when you find yourself in a bad place, but you do have one choice, and that choice is whether or not to fight, and in my opinion you have nothing to lose but everything to gain.

By Christmas 1996, the whole house was looking like a building site. Internally the dining room was adjacent to the kitchen, accessed through a glass door, and to the left of the door was a large serving hatch. The design of the interior and décor was all very typical of the 1960's style. It reminded me of something which you would imagine seeing on a set from the original TV adventure series of 'The Avengers', starring Steed and Mrs Peel. However, in its day, it would have been the envy of many, with its ultra modern exterior and interior.

Mrs Brooksbank used to reminisce about the flamboyant parties they used to throw, and I can imagine what a terrific house Bassett would have been to entertain in. With it's open plan design it would certainly lend itself to partying. Unfortunately, I don't think those parties had taken place for quite a few years as, sadly, Mr Brooksbank had not been a well man for some time before his death. Mrs Brooksbank had spoken of him often, and had nursed him for quite some time before he died. Obviously, from the way she had spoken, she had loved him a great deal. In some ways I felt very sad that the house had been left to deteriorate. Its walls would have been silent for so many years since the voices of happy laughter and chatter had been heard. But now we had the chance to bring it back to life, to give it back the sound of happy voices, and to give it back its character and the respect it deserved. It was in our hands, we were the new custodians, and we relished the opportunity to take on that responsibility.

The New Bassett House

By January 1997, the new build was very much in evidence - Bassett House was very much the Sharps' place. Walls, doors, fireplaces and new rooms were beginning to take shape, and it felt good to finally be seeing the fruits of our labour.

On the twenty-first day of March my mum and dad celebrated their golden wedding anniversary, fifty whole years of marriage. I dare say that during those fifty years they'd had many highs and many lows; that's life, I suppose you could say. On many occasions I still hear my dad's echoing voice saying to me, 'Aye lass, life's not a bed of roses. It can be very hard sometimes, but time's a big healer.' I've often thought how very true those words are.

We all celebrated with them at their local club. Many friends joined them to toast their achievement, and a good night was had by all. Little did we know how soon we would be experiencing life being hard!

Throughout the summer of '97 we pressed on in earnest with the renovation. The harder we worked the better it looked; the better it looked the harder we worked. We have been blessed with parents who have always taken an active role in supporting whatever project we have taken on, and Bassett was no exception.

Mums and dads came up at the weekend as usual. Saturdays were always a family day. Mums would sit and chat about anything and everything, and Nigel, his dad and me and my dad would always have some sort of project on: whether it be renovating Bassett, building a workshop for Nigel, digging out a fish pond or sorting the garden. Nigel and I were certainly not the gardening type, but both our dads were very keen gardeners, so we always turned to them for help and advice - in fact, for pretty much everything in those days.

Mums would make sandwiches at lunchtime, and give us a ten-minute warning so we could nip to the loo, wash our hands, and take our boots off. Then we'd sit around our large country kitchen table and put the world to rights. Invariably my dad used to leave the table first, as he never sat still for long, then the rest of us would follow. 'What's next on the agenda then, Bill?' my dad would say. Very early on with my relationship with Nigel, it was very clear that I was building a very close bond with Nigel's mum and dad. Over the years, they became like a second mum and dad to me, always treating me like a true daughter and never a daughter-in-law. They have always been there for me, they have looked after me throughout my various illnesses (boy there have been a few!), and they have been a shoulder to cry on at every hurdle. More importantly, they have always given me unconditional love.

Probably the most exciting part of the new build for me was one of the extensions that we had been fortunate enough to gain planning permission for: this was for our indoor swimming pool. Because of the ongoing problems with my back, I had found one sport that I could enjoy without too much discomfort, and swimming was also suggested by my consultant as helpful therapy.

The problem with me was that I couldn't just get into the pool and swim a gentle few lengths. Oh no, that wasn't my way; I had to swim as though I was training for a competition. I would put on my cap and goggles and set my stopwatch to time the session. Nigel used to get very irritated with me because I would just keep ploughing up and down the pool, and he'd want to stop every so often and have a chat. Consequently he used to say, 'Well, there's not much point me coming in with you, because you won't stop and I just get bored.'

I'd always been a decent swimmer, but I couldn't swim front crawl. Apparently front crawl is one of the best strokes for people with back problems, so Denise and I decided that we would enrol for swimming lessons to be taught front crawl. After 12 weeks my front crawl was pretty good, and so was Denise's: success! A very worthwhile exercise completed.

By completing much of the building work ourselves, the renovations and extensions became very laborious and time consuming. Nigel was determined to have the pool completed for my thirty-fourth birthday in October, which was looming up rapidly. Three weeks to spare, and we'd managed it. All we needed to do was to turn the tap on and start filling the pool with water. I can vividly remember the excitement and anticipation of nearing completion of the pool.

At last: I wouldn't have to drive to the leisure centre for my daily swim. What a luxury!

My mum and Nigel's mum both have September birthdays, the ninth and sixth respectively; so, as a joint celebration we invited them for tea, and thought it would be nice to celebrate the 'Official pool opening ceremony'.

It was a lovely day, the sun was shining, and as we all stood at the side of the pool, Nigel entered with a tray of six fluted glasses and a bottle of Champagne. The cork was popped open and we all cheered as we raised our glasses.

'Come on, Elaine, you can do the honours and turn on the tap,' Nigel smiled, 'after all, it's been done for you.'

I grinned, and happily strolled over to the tap. As I turned it on, Nigel quipped, 'We officially declare the pool open.'

Mums and dads clapped and we raised our glasses a second time.

The following morning, I was keen to see how much water was in the pool. Our bedroom is downstairs, so I nipped through the connecting door to take a look.

'Oh heck, it's not filling very quickly,' I shouted back to Nigel, who was still half asleep.

'How long will it take?' I shouted again. No answer.

'I say, Bun, (Bun is my pet name for Nigel), how long will it take?'

Still no answer: I tutted and climbed back into bed for another hour; after all, it was only 5.30am!

Thirty-six hours later, and I couldn't wait any longer. It was around 2.30pm on Sunday afternoon, and I was itching to get in the pool to test it out.

'Look, love,' Nigel sighed, 'there's barely enough water for you to swim in and, besides, it's going to be freezing. Remember, the water's coming straight from the tap; its cold water, you'll never swim in that.'

'Well, just how cold is it? I complained.

'Too cold!' he stated.

'Well, can't we take the temperature and just see how cold?' I replied.

'Oh, Elaine, can't you just wait for a few days until we can warm it up? You've waited this long, a few more days is not going to make any difference'.

'No, I can't. I want to swim today'.

'Ok, ok, you win, try it then. But it will be bloody cold!'

In no time at all I had changed into my swimming costume, and eagerly walked over to the steps which lowered into the pool. As I held onto the top of the handrail I looked towards Nigel, who had a knowing smile on his face.

My toes hit the water to an icy cold reception, and I mean ICY COLD!

'Ohhhhh, crikey,' I gasped.

'What was that?' shouted Nigel sarcastically. 'In you go then'.

'Maybe this wasn't such a good idea after all,' I thought.

I couldn't lose face now, though, not after all I'd said. I would just have to put up and shut up and get on with it.

'How's the water?' laughed Nigel. 'Having second thoughts yet?'

'Absolutely not,' I replied, 'no question of that!'

'Oh well, here goes,' I thought, as the competitive spirit in me took over. I wasn't going to be beaten, not now!

With a deep breath, I plunged my shoulders beneath the water. For a second or two it felt like the air was being pumped out of me, but I soon realised it was just my body in shock from the coldness of the water. I struggled for a while to catch my breath, but eventually my body adjusted to the temperature. Two lengths, two lengths, I thought, just manage two lengths! Towards the end of the second length, I could no longer feel my fingertips or my toes, but it didn't matter, because I'd beaten the challenge.

Depression

I had never been very sympathetic when people discussed depression, probably because I'd never experienced it - or so I thought!

However, throughout periods of my teenage years I experienced spells of feeling very sad inside, my heart would feel heavy and I found myself feeling really tearful. I didn't like this feeling, but there again I didn't understand it. Why did I feel like this? I felt bad, I felt like I'd done something wrong, but what? Why?

Three weeks after we'd received the news that I would need Chemotherapy, I hit the brick wall as I refer to it.

I'd been so brave up to this point, being strong for everybody else. Now I felt like I was letting myself down. All the English stiff upper lip rubbish, and I was about to fall to pieces. The truth is though, that I wasn't worrying about the cancer; I certainly didn't feel I was. I could feel myself becoming more and more insular. I didn't want to see anybody, let alone talk to anyone. I just wanted Nigel to hold me and tell me I was going to be okay. The tension was unbearable. My head felt like it was about to explode. Voices in my head were constantly picking at me but I was so, so tired. I just wanted to rest, I just wanted to sleep and find peace. Oh, just to rest, I wanted it more than anything. I was constantly asking Nigel for reassurance, not about the cancer, just about me!

It's strange, but looking back at my teenage years, I knew in my heart of hearts that one day it would all come to a head. Just how it would come to a head is what I didn't know, and actually I didn't realise when the trigger was finally pulled until some months later. Nigel had always coped remarkably well with my many issues with ill health up to this point, but I don't think even Nigel could have anticipated just what was going to be required of him to pull us through this one. Much lesser men would have walked away before now, but it is with his unconditional love for me that he held my hand every step of the way.

Nigel had realised, after a few days, that this seemingly 'low period' was much more serious than that. My appetite reduced dramatically, and with that so did my energy resources. My weight plummeted and I was permanently tired. I didn't want to go out of the house, I didn't want to talk, and I spent so much time just staring into space, as though I was in a trance. Nigel would try to end the silence by snapping his fingers in front of my face and nudging me. He'd shout my name out of frustration, just to try to get a response from me; but there was none. I know he felt helpless and desperately wanted to help me, but he was struggling to know who to ask for advice. In previous years when Nigel had suggested perhaps seeing a doctor I'd broken down in tears and said, 'How can I tell a doctor what's inside my head? I can't, I just can't, he'll think I'm insane.' I'd always made Nigel promise that he would never force me to see a doctor, and so with all this in mind you can imagine his predicament. He tried everything he could with me, talking through my worries, trying to reason through the issues, trying to understand how I felt, but by this stage I was struggling to put a sentence together, let alone hold a reasonable conversation.

Nigel came to the conclusion that he needed to take action, and so he rang Mr Shorthouse, who put him in touch with a psychologist. An appointment was organised for her to visit me, and she made a home visit to Bassett the following day. In hindsight, this was the beginning of a very slow and painful black tunnel with no chink of daylight for weeks and months to follow. I know it sounds a little bit like a cliché but, probably the best way to explain it, is like trying to climb a mountain without any equipment. When I'd almost got my fingertips gripping the top, it felt like someone just kicked me right back down to the bottom. Again I was back to square one and had to start all over again. For several months Nigel would take me to see Louise (psychologist) at her home, in the hope that my depression would ease and lift, but it didn't. At times it was just static, but at times it worsened.

Between Christmas and New Year of 1997 Nigel had, after much persuasion, got me to agree to travel with him to the Isle of Dogs on the Thames. He had been looking to buy a small John Deere 755 tractor for some time, to help him with the ongoing renovations we were doing at Bassett. He had placed a 'wanted ad' in one of the agricultural magazines, and was contacted by this chap based on the Isle of Dogs. The only problem was, he wanted us to go to look at the tractor, and possibly collect it, before he and his family went away on holiday on New Year's Eve. The seller had had a great deal of interest in the tractor, and was eager to have it collected ASAP. Nigel tried his best to express to me what a good buy it seemed. The working hours were low, and from all the photos that he had of the tractor, it seemed to be just what he was looking for. In the end I agreed to go, but it was a bit of a disaster, apart from Nigel coming home with his tractor. I had severe bouts of sobbing whilst travelling in the car, I felt so desperately sad. I was like a little girl who couldn't be consoled; if only I could find some peace in a different place. When people talk about feeling suicidal, I think I can honestly say I've been there. I wanted out, and I felt the time bomb was ticking!

We returned home on a Friday evening to another difficult situation. Whilst we had been away, the weather had been bitterly cold, and as soon as we entered Bassett we were greeted by the sound of running water. We'd had a pipe burst!

What you first have to understand is that three of our bedrooms are downstairs, one of which is ours. We had completed the refurb. of our bedroom and en suite, and two months previously had had a brand new pale green carpet fitted. The carpet was no longer fitted…, it was afloat, along with our bed!

I was stood at the top of the staircase in the dining room, just stunned with what I saw.

What a mess! It looked like a scene from the comedy film, 'The Money Pit' (starring Tom Hanks, it's the story of a magnificent house purchased by a young couple that begins to fall to pieces as soon as they move in).

I was horrified. All the work we had done, and now this. My legs went to jelly, my head began to spin, and I collapsed on the spot.

Nigel picked me up and sat me on a chair in the kitchen. With my head in my hands, resting on the table, I began to sob uncontrollably. Nigel rang his parents and my parents, who immediately said they were on there way up to Bassett. Under any normal circumstances I would have been in there working alongside Nigel and our dads in the clean up, but not this time. I was mentally and physically incapable. Our mums did their best to console me, but to be honest I think they felt totally helpless to know what to do with me. Looking back, it must have been horrendous for my loved ones. I don't suppose as a parent you ever expect to have to face the possibility of losing a daughter or a son to a cancer, but not only were all four parents having to face that thought, they were also having to deal with all the other crap that was happening.

As for Nigel: well, does anyone imagine losing their thirty-four year old wife? To this day I am still in absolute awe of how he stood by me. To have coped with what he has, is of immense credit to him. People talk about 'Love' so flippantly. Nigel's love has shown 'Love' beyond comprehension; how much can one man take before he himself breaks?

Throughout all of this Nigel has never ever wavered in front of me; maybe in his quiet moments quite possibly, but I never was in any doubt that he would be by my side for the long haul and, my God, what a long haul it's been!

Black Hole

Misery, sheer hell: that's what comes to mind when I think of that time. Days slipped into weeks, and the weeks turned into months. No change: I was living in my own prison and no one could reach me, not even Nigel. I felt like I had reached the point of no return. Is this the way I would exist? If it was then I didn't want to. I wanted peace. Endless sleep - surely - would find me endless peace.

I've heard some people comment on committing suicide, and what their opinions on it are.

Some people are sympathetic and try to understand what a bad place one must be in to contemplate doing such a thing. Yet I've heard some people say its selfish, and a coward's way out. To be honest, I struggle to see how some people can think the latter.

From my experience, it's not a question of making a considered decision; that doesn't even come into the equation. I found myself struggling to string a sentence together. In my opinion, one is not of sane mind when in such a bad place. I know this sounds so dramatic, and I do not mean to infer that physical illness is inferior to mental illness, but every part of my being felt numb and blank. I didn't want to talk to anyone, or even see any members of my family. If the phone rang I would sob uncontrollably, and Nigel would need to hold me and tell me it would be okay. I didn't want to get out of bed in the mornings. Nigel had to literally drag me out of bed and physically stand me in the shower to wash me; otherwise I wouldn't have bothered. He would switch the shower on and empty shampoo onto my hair, lift my hand and show me how to rub my head to wash my hair. Next he would soap the sponge to bathe me, lift up my arms to wash my armpits and then work his way downwards, until finally finishing with my feet. I was just a dummy who was moved from one place to the next. My world was virtually non existent. I know now, without a shadow of a doubt, that if I hadn't had the love and support of Nigel and my family, I would definitely not be here today. I'm not proud of that fact, but neither am I ashamed.

Although our twice weekly visit to see my psychologist did seem to help, progress was extremely slow, and it was rare for me to go from one visit to the next without making a couple of phone calls to Louise for help. It was at one of the weekly visits that Louise was very open and honest with Nigel and myself and, although I didn't fully understand what this would mean, I was in no position to question her decision. 'Actually, Nigel, I think I need to put my cards on the table, and tell you that I think I've gone as far as I possibly can with Elaine now. I believe that further treatment will be necessary if Elaine is ever to be fully well, and I'm afraid it would not be ethical for me to continue treating Elaine under these circumstances'.

The following week, an appointment had been made for us to see a consultant psychiatrist at Sheffield's Claremont Hospital.

It was 4.50pm on a Saturday afternoon, in the spring of 1998. We were shown into a private room, where a short man with a beard sat behind a desk. As we approached he stood up and held out his hand. Nigel shook his hand and thanked him for seeing us at such short notice, then introduced me. He turned to look at me, again held out his hand and said, 'Hello, Elaine, please take a seat.' I sat on a grey upholstered chair on Nigel's right-hand side, and I wore the same black blazer and grey slacks which I had worn when we visited Mr Shorthouse only a few months earlier.

The exact sequence of events which then took place is not all that clear in my mind, which is strange because for most occasions I can recall memories word for word. Now, whether that is because it was, and still is, very painful to think about, I'm not sure. Perhaps it is my mind's way of blocking out so many years of living with, and trying to deal with, such a debilitating mental illness, which I had never even heard of, let alone understand until our meeting with Dr Macaskill that spring day.

OCD

(Obsessive-Compulsive Disorder)

Obsessive-Compulsive Disorder shows itself in many different forms.

OCD is an anxiety disorder characterised by intrusive thoughts that produce uneasiness, apprehension, fear or worry, by repetitive behaviours aimed at reducing the associated anxiety, or by a combination of such obsessions and compulsions. Symptoms of the disorder can include excessive washing or cleaning, repeated checking, extreme hoarding, or preoccupation with sexual, violent or religious thoughts. Some people with OCD also develop depression and severe depression, and may sometimes have suicidal thoughts and feelings.

The diagram below shows how obsessions and compulsions are connected in an OCD cycle.

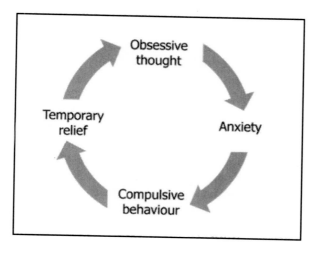

If you experience OCD, your obsessions and compulsions will cause you considerable fear and distress. They will also take up a significant amount of time, and disrupt your ability to carry on with your day-to-day to life, including doing daily chores, going to work, or maintaining relationships with friends and family.

Many people with OCD experience feelings of shame and loneliness. This often stops them from seeking help, particularly if they experience distressing thoughts about subjects such as religion, sex or violence.

This means that many people try to cope with OCD alone, until the symptoms are so severe that they can't hide them any more. OCD is also known to have a close association with depression, and some people find obsessions appear, or become worse, when they are depressed.

Some psychology theories suggest that OCD is caused by personal experience. It is thought that if you have had a painful childhood experience, or suffered trauma or abuse, you might learn to use obsessions and compulsions to cope with anxiety. However, this theory does not explain why people who cannot point to any painful experiences might experience OCD.

Many people who know me will probably be surprised to discover that I have OCD. Over the early years (from the age of 13) I was able to hide it from the outside world. Even my family wasn't aware. To be honest, even I wasn't aware. It was my secret that that I had to hide. Over the years my OCD worsened. I felt so alone, frightened, ashamed and disgusted about what I had in my head. I've been told by experts that it was the diagnosis of cancer that was the catalyst for it all finally coming to a head. It's been horrendous and it's something that I have had to learn to deal with and live with on a daily basis. With the love and support of Nigel, family, friends and, of course, my animals, we get through it. Over the years of treatment, the good days now out-weigh the bad days, but I am never so naïve as to think that I'm cured. I will always live in a certain amount of fear of it returning, as it has done on so many occasions. In fact, I'll probably take that fear to my grave. I know it sounds ridiculous for most people to accept, but I feel that, if it hadn't been for the diagnosis of cancer, the OCD may not have been forced to the surface, and I may still be living in a very different world of my own. I have cancer to thank for facing OCD, and finally getting the treatment I so desperately needed. However, for anyone out there who is suffering, you really don't need to suffer alone. Help is out there. Believe me, it took twenty-one years for me to finally seek help. Please, don't waste even one year, let alone twenty-one years!

Fighting Back

George and I sharing a tender moment

It's not been easy. It still isn't easy and in fact it's been the hardest challenge I've ever had to face; much harder than fighting the cancer. Even today I still have 'blips'. However, the key to coping and dealing with OCD is recognising the trigger, which in itself can be difficult. If the thoughts and pictures are really severe and intrusive, then it can be too debilitating to even recognise the signs. Nigel is fantastic with me though, and always gives me his undivided attention to talk it through.

The mind is incredible, but it can also be very dangerous and frightening. I have so much empathy with anyone who may be trying to deal with this horrible illness. I would not wish this on my worst enemy. My main aim for writing this book is because, if I can help just one person who may be trying to deal with this illness, then it will have been worth it. As you already now know, the illness manifested itself many years ago, although we didn't know it was an illness until we were introduced to Dr Mackaskill.

I suppose after that I did take some comfort in the knowledge that I was suffering from a recognised and documented illness. Living with OCD can be a very difficult subject to talk about. It can be embarrassing, distressing and completely take over your life at times. I know, because I live with it twenty-four seven, three hundred and sixty-five days a year. No two individuals' circumstances are the same, and I know that I've been blessed with an incredible husband and family. Without them my situation could have been far worse, and I feel tremendously saddened for people less fortunate than me, who are dealing with this awful illness alone.

Living with mental illness can be a very lonely life, because to everyone else it's not visible, it's difficult to understand, and the subject matter can be difficult to talk about for the patient and their loved ones. The one thing I can tell you, is that there are people who can and will help you. Together with the help of a psychiatrist, medication and cognitive therapy, there will be some light at the end of your dark tunnel, but it will take some time. It's not an easy road to travel. It's tough and it's very tiring at times but, unless you take the first steps, you'll never find out.

Turning Point

From the age of four years old I have always had a fascination with Llamas. This all started with our annual family holiday in Blackpool. Over the week that we spent there, every year, I always looked forward to our trip to the famous Blackpool Pleasure Beach. For any of you who don't know what the Pleasure Beach consists of, I'll explain. It's a huge area of amusement rides that stretches over several miles. Children and adults alike love the thrill of the daring roller coaster ride, known as the 'Big Dipper', as well as the 'Grand National', where two carriages appear to challenge each other to the race. The 'Log flume' was another great ride. Sitting in what appeared to be a log (plastic actually), and racing around a water-filled flowing canal, gave me hours of pure pleasure. The 'Big Horses' was another ride. I suppose it could be described as Lancashire's answer to Disney World. Candy floss came in abundance, along with hot dogs, doughnuts and kiss-me-quick hats. I loved it.

One particular year I spotted an unusual looking animal, quite big and furry, with banana-shaped ears and a pointy face. Little did I know it then, but it was a Llama. I can remember tugging at dad's hand to take me over for a closer look; it was magical. Its long, dark eyelashes were beautiful, yet it stood so regally and proud. That was it. I was smitten. Llama rides were being offered to small children, as well as pony rides, but it was the llama that I wanted. It was smartly groomed in all its traditional dress, and I will never forget the excitement I felt when dad sat me on that saddle. To this day, that initial picture and excitement I felt on that special occasion has stayed with me.

By now it was late March 1999 and, although I was still in the relatively early stages of my recovery, I felt I was in need of a focus. Unfortunately, in February I had found a further breast lump, which needed to be removed asap. Because of my mental state, it was deemed that the chemotherapy should be delayed for one month. It was a Sunday afternoon and, as usual, Nigel and I were relaxing in our lounge together. For some strange reason I picked up Nigel's 'Farming Magazine', which is something I never did, and started to flick through the ads. I'm still not sure what must have been going through my mind, but one of the ads, in bold black letters, stated, 'Llamas for sale'. It was almost as if a switch had been turned on.

'Nigel, Nigel,' I said, as I got to my feet. 'That's it. I've got it.'

'Got what?' he asked.

'Llama, llama, that's what I want. That's what I need.'

Nigel stared back at me in amazement, trying to determine if I had said what he thought he had heard me say.

'Look, love, hang on a minute. Just think this through. You can't just go and buy a llama.'

'Why not?' I replied. 'There's some for sale. Look at this,' I said, as I walked over and pushed the magazine into his hand.

'Love, you've got to start chemo soon. That's not going to be easy, so we certainly don't need to start adding a llama to our commitments.'

'But don't you see, bun, this could be just what I need. A focus, an animal that needs me to care for it, a distraction from the treatment. It could be the making of me.'

'It might also be a disaster,' he sighed, knowing that he'd already lost the battle. At this time in our life, Nigel would have given me anything, anything to see me smile again and make me happy. Nigel has said since, that he had no idea what the following months and years might bring. Would the cancer return? Would he still have his wife in five years time? All questions he just couldn't answer, and for that reason he would have given me anything I wanted, no matter how bizarre! And so the seed was sown. All I had to do now was to do some research and make a few phone calls.

Extraordinary bond between human and Llama. Marty and me.
Summer 1998

Finding Marty and Georgie

I think the consensus of opinion within my family was one of astonishment when I told them about my llama idea. I'm sure thoughts of 'unstable' and 'well, it must be because of the shock', must have been considered by them at some stage. After all, it's not everyone who would choose to buy a llama. Let's just say, 'It's not the norm, is it?' But then, I'm not the norm! Anyhow, no matter what they thought or said, they went along with me and gave me their support, as they have always done.

Whilst researching the needs and requirements of llamas, I came across another member of the camelid family, who looked just as drop dead gorgeous as the llama.

Enter, Alpaca!

Slightly smaller in height and build, alpacas are very similar to their relatives (llamas), but they have a much denser, and finer fleece. Llamas have much more coarse fibre which is guard hair (rougher). Hence llama fibre is lower quality than alpaca fibre, but both animals are equally gorgeous.

During the research process, I discovered that llamas and alpacas are herd animals and therefore cannot live alone, but the day to day husbandry and care required is the same for both; likewise the feeding and dietary requirements.

Okay, okay, now one makes two does it? Oh well, I'm sure Nigel will go with that… I hoped! Sure enough, I was reluctantly given the nod. Decision made, it was to be one llama and one alpaca, purely because I'd fallen in love with them both!

After talking to endless alpaca and llama breeders over the following few days, I eventually felt confident enough to choose the two breeders who I wanted to purchase my animals from. The llama breeder was based in Ascot, very near to the horse racing track, and the alpaca breeder was based near Reading, just inside

Oxfordshire. I'd made arrangements for Nigel and me to travel down the following weekend, to take a look at the animals that were available for sale. Nigel had suggested that we should stay overnight in a hotel, so we could visit each breeder for a day, to enable us to take time looking at the animals; so we would be equipped to make the right decision. It would also be time out for the two of us to relax and make a nice weekend of it. It had seemed such a long time since I'd had something nice to think about, and it felt good.

Our first port of call was Ascot, where the llama farm was. A larger-than-life american lady greeted us with a huge smile, and took us towards the field where some llamas were grazing. Her farm/country residence was a beautiful place. She was a keen horsewoman, and she proudly introduced me to her trusty steed. He was a lovely boy, a dark bay warmblood, with a stunning head. I asked her how old he was. He was a seven-year-old that she had brought on from a youngster, and was now eventing him. I felt a tinge of envy, as I had always dreamed of one day owning my own horse, and I thought how lucky she was to have so much. She owned several horses that had been with her many years, but she said she couldn't bear to sell them on, as they were part of her family now, and they would remain with her the rest of their lives. At that time, I didn't have the passion for animals that I have now, but I now get what she meant, because I too have that love and passion for my four legged friends.

The field where the llamas were kept opened on to several larger paddocks, with different groups of llamas in them. She explained that all her 'girls and boys' ran separately, only coming together when it was mating time. Alpacas and llamas are unusual animals, in that they are induced ovulators. This means that it's specifically the act of copulation that stimulates the release of an egg follicle; therefore they can become pregnant any time of the year, and they don't have a season like sheep and other animals do. I was now beginning to realise that I had a great deal to learn but, on the flip side of the coin, that was not a bad thing, as my mind would be occupied with something other than chemo.

It was a bitterly cold day, but crisp and dry with sunshine making the occasional appearance. The group that we were interested in were the boys that had just been weaned. Normally, at the age of six months, mum and baby (dam and cria) are separated for the weaning process. Depending on the size and weight of the cria, this can also be done at five months of age. Sometimes, mum will self wean, and kick off her baby when she feels it's the right time. What you need to know here is, that because their gestation period is fifty weeks, most dams are pregnant again for the following season. As a result, they are using up a lot of energy (calories) feeding the new foetus and themselves, and generally trying to keep warm, so the sooner their cria become self sufficient, the better it is for them. However, some dams are very generous and will keep feeding their cria until us humans intervene. As we wandered through the field looking at all the different llamas available, I noticed the shadow of something moving inside a field shelter. As I peered around the opening, another face was looking back at me. Big, round, brown eyes stared into mine. Oh, those eyelashes, long, dark and luscious, absolutely drop-dead gorgeous: this was my first encounter with Marty, who would soon become my own. He stood proud and confident, and gave out a little hum as I stepped forward towards him. He backed further into the corner of the shelter, and this time gave out a little snort as if to say, 'Okay, that's close enough.' I stepped back, not wanting to unnerve him, as he lifted his head into the air. He looked arrogant, and turned his head sideways on to me, as though acknowledging his prowess and stature.

From that moment on I was smitten. I wanted him. Wow: what an unbelievable creature! In those final few moments of meeting him, something had passed between us in mutual respect.

Now, on the other hand, 'Georgie' was completely different. Right from the very first time I set eyes on him he was needy. He stuck very close to his mum and continually hummed to her, and she reciprocated, to reassure him that he was okay. He was just one great bundle of dark brown fluff with a little black face, nose and big eyes somewhere in the middle of all the fluff. His little spear-shaped black ears pointed out just above his topknot (the mass of heaped, wavy fibre on an alpaca's head). He was so very different from Marty, but I new instantly he was the one for me.

'What do you think? He's so sweet and pretty,' I said, as I looked at Nigel for his agreement. 'It's your choice, love, it's entirely up to you.' They say opposites attract and, over the weeks and months to come, Marty and Georgie became really good for each other, and for me. They became my soul mates.

New Lease of Life

I knew I'd always been searching for something. I just didn't know what that something was. There was a part of my being that wasn't complete and content.

I desperately loved Nigel, I had a fantastic family who had been so supportive throughout the depression and OCD; what more did I want or need? Something was just eluding me, and I felt unable to find the final piece of the jigsaw. I didn't know whether I would ever find that something, because I didn't know what I was searching for. I just had this overwhelming feeling of being incomplete. To this day I still find it sad, that I never felt I fulfilled my dad's dream of becoming an Olympian. It's sad, because I do believe that I had the talent and ability and I know many other people in the athletic fraternity believed that as well. The problem was me! I mean, inside me! To be the best you have to want it so, so badly. I did want the success, but I wanted the success for someone else, and that someone was 'my dad'. I'm sure that everyone involved in top class athletics will tell you that you need to want it for yourself. That was my failing; I didn't, and my heart wanted the success for dad. Again, I still believe that my dad was robbed of an Olympic medal all those years ago, and I so much wanted to give him that medal back through my achievements. Dad deserved that, and as long as I live I will always be saddened that I was unable to do that for my dad.

What I do hope is that, over the past sixteen years, dad can be proud of what I have achieved in a far different sphere from sport and, by that, I mean 'Mayfield Alpacas'!

When Georgie and Marty came into my life, I was given 'a new lease of life'.

I didn't realise at the time that this was the elusive piece of the jigsaw. The 'something' I'd been searching for was at the tip of my fingers and boy was I about to grab it!

We had to wait several long weeks before we could take delivery of Marty and Georgie, due to the fact that they were not old enough to be weaned from their dams (mums) when we initially chose them. We also had to get the timing right to ensure that we had their correct housing in position for welcoming them into their new home. Both alpacas and llamas can cope with temperatures as low as minus fifteen if the weather remains dry, but due to the lack of lanolin in their fibre they cannot cope with prolonged wet conditions and low temperatures, as they are not waterproof like sheep and ducks are, and so they cannot shed the water. The rain could chill through to their bodies and cause them to shiver, hence the need for shelter in wet conditions. However, they are very hardy creatures and have learned to survive high in the Andes on the barren 'Antiplano' on a very sparse low protein diet. They are very intelligent creatures and quite resilient, contrary to what people may think.

At last, the day finally arrived when we were able to collect them. Again we booked into a hotel the previous night near to where our first pick-up was, so we could get an early start the following day. It would be a long one, and Nigel wanted to make sure that we could drive back up north to Bassett and arrive to unload the animals in daylight. Also, I had just started my chemotherapy and it was proving difficult, making me feel rather sleepy and unwell at times. Nigel didn't want anything to spoil my enjoyment on collecting them, as for the first time in a long time I had become exited and focused about their arrival. Ascot, and Marty was our first pick up. We arrived early at 'Ordellamas', the lady breeder was called Ordell, an American name by all accounts. To our amusement we arrived just in time to see Ordell trotting round the ménage on one of her, no, not horses…llamas! Yes, that's right, no joke, although it did look like something out of a scene from a comedy sketch at the time!

Ordell is a slight lady, like me, and Isaac (stud male) was a big guy, very large, tall and stocky and quite capable of carrying

Ordell's slight frame. It's just not what you expect to see being ridden round a ménage, is it? Horse, yes: llama, no!

To my surprise, Marty loaded into the trailer really well. He was a little concerned about being alone, but not really as upset as I had expected: so far, so good. Ordell and I gave each other a hug. Over the past weeks we had talked a great deal over the phone and seemed to get on very well. I liked her a lot. Nigel had briefly explained to Ordell about my illness and the start of chemo. I think Nigel was concerned that I was taking too much on, bearing in mind what I had ahead of me, and he just looked to Ordell for some sort of reassurance. Looking back now, I realise that I was at a very vulnerable stage in my treatment. Nigel knew that and, to be fair, I think Ordell did too. The one resounding piece of advice she gave me was, 'Just remember, Elaine, I know he's cuddly, but he's also a llama. Don't forget to treat him like one.' Little did I envisage how that advice would come back to haunt me fourteen months later but, at the time, as far as I was concerned, this was just the tonic that I needed and I couldn't get enough of it.

New Arrivals

Once again, Georgie proved to be the needy one. It wasn't difficult to load him into the trailer, because Nigel just picked him up and placed him inside with Marty. It was when we got him in the trailer that the problems started. It appeared that Georgie had not really been separated from his dam (mum) for very long and was still finding the transition to being on his own difficult. In hindsight it must have been quite traumatic for the poor little fellow. Sixteen years on, I certainly would not allow a young weanling to leave my farm, unless it had been weaned from mum for several weeks. The weaning process can be very stressful for both mum and cria, and at times of stress weanlings can be very susceptible to ill health due to their immune system becoming compromised. Therefore, I prefer this process to be achieved over several weeks. This allows me to monitor both weanling and dam for any signs of ill thrift, (i.e. separation from the group, loss of appetite, which ultimately causes weight loss).

Once we had left Georgie's birth place, we tracked back cross country to continue the four-and-a-half hour journey back to Sheffield. At convenient places along the way we pulled in to check our cargo. Marty appeared to be quite nonchalant about the whole thing. Every time I peeked over the trailer back he was in cush position (sitting down) and didn't quite seem to understand what Georgie was making all the fuss about. Georgie was humming constantly, in a high pitch tone, and pacing around the trailer as if he was searching for an escape route. Knowing what I know now, he definitely had all the symptoms of a really stressed alpaca. It upset me to see him like that, but I didn't know what I could do to make his situation better.

'Elaine, he'll settle, stop worrying, it's just all new for him. The more we stop will probably be making him worse. Let's just crack on up the motorway and get home,' said Nigel.

Reluctantly I agreed, jumped back in the 4x4 and sat tight until we finally reached Bassett. As we approached our drive I could see mums and dads stood by our paddock gate awaiting the new arrivals. It was a Saturday and, as mums and dads spent every Saturday with us, we had rung on ahead to let them know our ETA. At the bottom of our drive we had installed a second-hand cattle grid, which Nigel had picked up at a bargain price. We had fenced the dedicated paddock for the animals, but Nigel was concerned that, if they did escape the paddock, they could possibly negotiate their way out onto Bassett Lane, and then we would be in a mess! Can you imagine the double takes you would get from walkers and car drivers having sight of a free range llama and alpaca taking a stroll around the Mayfield Valley?

At last we were home. Nigel reversed the trailer into position, and the moment had arrived to introduce Marty and Georgie to their new home. Nigel opened the trailer door, and I was so exited I was skipping around like an eight-year-old. The ramp was lowered to the ground and there, at the back of the trailer, stood two very shy, little creatures looking back at us all. I swear I felt my heart skip a beat!

'Oohs' and 'ahs' continued for what seemed like a couple of minutes. Nigel put his arm around my shoulder, smiling as he pulled me towards him saying, 'Is this what you wanted? Are you happy, girl?' I beamed a wide grin as I nuzzled my head into his chest and quietly said, 'Thank you. I love you.'

Marty was the first one to sound a gentle hum. Georgie, being smaller than Marty, looked up to Marty for reassurance, then looked back at us. Although Marty and Georgie looked a little bemused at the four faces staring back at them, so too was I.

This was all new for me too. I only had knowledge of what I'd read in the interim period, between choosing the boys, up until collecting them. Admittedly, I'd read virtually twenty-four seven in that short space of time, but reading is certainly no substitute for hands-on experience. I didn't come from a farming background. My uncle Stan (my Dads brother) was a farmer, but only on a very small scale. The farm only consisted of seven acres, on which uncle Stan ran a very small dairy herd and a few sheep. I had always enjoyed spending time on the farm. As a child the farm was of great fascination, with all the hidey holes to explore and the haystack to climb. I was quite a brave child and, to Denise's horror, I would climb any ladders that might look like they led to anywhere interesting. Denise was terrified of heights. I can see her now, standing at the bottom of the haystack, pleading for me to come down and be careful. I was in my element though, and sometimes used to tease her that I was falling. Denise, as usual, always looked out for me and those times on the farm were no different. All the family, mum, dad, Sylv, Denise and I always helped out at the farm when the potatoes were ready to be picked; it was an annual event for us.

One year in particular I can remember the chaos that was caused by dad's car. Dad had parked the car outside one of the fields that we were picking from. Uncle Stan had wanted dad to use the car as a collection point for the two fields which we were working on, but dad didn't like the idea of taking the car into the field, in case we got stuck between the ruts that had been ploughed. After some discussion between dad and Uncle Stan, dad was persuaded that the car would be fine to drive into the field.

It's strange how vividly I can remember that day. We had a navy-blue Vauxhall Viva, registration number WWE 272G. It proved to be that dad's car in Uncle Stan's field was a bad idea after all!

Unfortunately, Uncle Stan had not taken into consideration how little clearance there was underneath the car. Yep, as guessed, we got stuck! The prop shaft looked like some futuristic machine designed to collect potatoes! What a mess! Uncle Stan's name was mud for the remainder of the day. Looking back, it makes me chuckle to visualise the scene. 'Bloody hell, Stan, I said it was a bad idea,' snapped dad, as he crawled underneath the car to see what the damage was. 'Many hands make light work,' as the saying goes, and in this case that's just what happened. An eventful day that was never repeated again on potato picking day!

In at the Deep End

The day after we had collected 'the boys' was a Sunday. The weather was awful, rain, rain and more rain. I awoke early as I was keen to go and see the boys. I hoped that they had been sensible enough to use the field shelter we had made for them, but no, they hadn't. The straw had not been disturbed at all. Once again my lack of experience showed. When I sell any of my alpacas to customers, I always tell them not to be concerned if the alpacas don't use their field shelter for a week or so. Alpacas are quite timid creatures and have to be confident and comfortable in their new surroundings before venturing into new shelters. Alpacas are, however, very nosey creatures, and eventually curiosity will get the better of them and they will start to explore their new surroundings. Once they've checked things out, peered into the shelter a few times, and had one foot inside, they will eventually decide that its okay, and actually, yeah, its better to be in here than stood outside in the rain.

By lunchtime it was still raining. As I stood in our lounge looking out through the window, I was sure they were shivering. Nigel was laid on the sofa watching TV, totally oblivious to what was happening outside. That was until I decided that enough was enough. I was fretting at them stood in the rain. 'Nigel, I'm worried about the boys, they look cold'. No answer came from the sofa. 'Nigel, did you hear me?' I said.

'They look cold. Why aren't they inside the shelter?'

'Er, well, they obviously don't want to'.

'Nigel, Nigel, look at them, we've got to do something'.

'Like what? he sighed, sounding really not bothered. 'Look, love, I'm trying to watch the Grand Prix'.

'Oh, Nigel, please come and help me get them in, I can't manage on my own…please,' I pleaded.

'It's hopeless, totally useless, the one thing I look forward to once a fortnight on a Sunday. But no, you want me to go running round the paddock in the pouring rain, chasing after a llama and an alpaca. It's crazy, Elaine, just crazy!'

Ten minutes later a reluctant Nigel, still complaining, followed me into the paddock where the boys were. 'So, what now? What's the plan? How do we get them in the shelter?' Nigel said, sarcastically. 'Well…well, let's think,' I said stalling for time. 'What do you suggest?' 'Oh no, no, this is your idea, you decide,' said Nigel, as he threw his arms in the air.

Some two hours later we triumphantly shot the bolt across the bottom half of the stable door behind the two boys. Both of us leaned against the door, absolutely knackered, trying to catch our breath. The rain was still pouring down, but by now we didn't really notice or even care. Although Nigel would never ever admit it, I do believe he did feel some satisfaction when we finally got them tucked up with food and water in their nice warm dry bed!

Those first few months, owning Marty and Georgie was a massive learning curve for me. It certainly had its highs and lows. I was trying to cope with the trauma which chemo brings, but at the same time I was totally responsible for the two beautiful creatures standing outside in our paddock. Nigel had made it quite clear that if I was going to go ahead with taking on a llama and an alpaca then 'on my head be it'. They would be my sole responsibility, and I had to look after and care for them. Some people might think Nigel sounded quite hard saying this to me, but Nigel knows me better than anybody. He knew that this would probably give me the focus which I needed to help pull me through the dreadful depression and OCD. Don't get me wrong; those early days were very, very difficult at times. My whole demeanour was like an ever-changing pendulum, sometimes it would be swinging in a good direction, but at other times it was stationary in the wrong direction. Throughout it all I had a duty, a duty to the two beautiful animals that graced our paddock. No matter how bad I felt, whether caused by the chemo or the depression, I still had to get out of bed to care for Marty and Georgie. They needed me; I was their life-line, and they needed me to be there for them no matter what. The one lasting memory of those early days was that, no matter how bad I felt, Marty and Georgie always managed to make me smile and, to be honest, I think that was pretty damned good.

As spring turned into summer I was gaining more confidence handling my boys. I had taught them to walk on a head collar, but ironically it was Marty who proved to be the awkward one on this occasion. Like most animals alpacas have a short concentration span when learning new tasks; so little and often is the best way to teach them. Sixteen years ago alpacas where still pretty rare in the UK, especially where we lived, which made moral support from other owners virtually non-existent. Nigel was always on hand to lend an ear but, apart from that, I was pretty much on my own. Neither family nor friends had a clue about these so-called camelids, so it was down to me and trial and error. The first time I ventured out of our paddock with them was fairly non-eventful, not at all what I had imagined. With one in each hand I walked them up our drive towards the front door. It was a Saturday and a lovely warm summer's day. Mums and dads were with us as usual, so I thought we would surprise them and ring the door bell. Nigel and dads were working in the garden on their latest project and, as we smugly sauntered past them, they cheered and gave us a round of applause!

I knew mums were busy in the kitchen making elevenses coffee for us all, so the three of us wandered towards the front door and rang the bell. A few seconds later I could hear footsteps approaching. 'Just a minute,' said a voice that I recognised as my mum's. 'Ok, don't rush,' I shouted back. The door opened and a stunned mum looked out. 'Well, I never,' gasped mum. 'Sheila, Sheila, come here. Look who's come to see us'. Sure enough, Nigel's mum followed with a wide grin appearing on her face! 'Goodness me,' exclaimed an equally surprised mum.

Cruel Sea

It takes no prisoners. It demands respect. A stormy sea is dangerous, dark, cold and menacing. It can take lives without thought or concern or remorse. It's a foaming mass of anger just waiting to draw you closer and then swallow you up when you can fight no more. It's reminiscent of OCD and depression. In short, the word 'terrifying' describes it best!

Unless you've lived through the experience, you will never ever know just how bad it is. To quote a well-known term, 'Just when you think it's safe to go back in the water'; how very true that is.

I know, because I lived through the experience and continue to do so, on a daily basis. Just like the sea, I have my controlled, settled, calm days and weeks, but I can never be sure when another storm may whip up. Maybe I will never be sure; maybe I will take this fear with me to my grave; maybe is the future, and the future is totally unknown.

With Marty and Georgie I was beginning to find some sort of contentment. I was several months into my chemo, when another storm was brewing. We were still in the very early stages of understanding the illness, and what to look for in the tell-tale signs; but I knew I wasn't okay. I felt a familiar black cloud descending on me rapidly. I couldn't run away from it, because it seemed to be attached to me by elastic. I was frightened, and shrinking back into my shell. My medication had recently been changed. In the early days of long-term medication it was important to experiment with a few different combinations to see what worked best. I was taking a cocktail of drugs, and all of them had different side effects. Whenever I went to Western Park for my treatment, some member of the family went with me. I would have been absolutely fine on my own, but everyone wanted to give me their individual support, and be with me at some point throughout the therapy.

This particular day, Nigel's mum and dad had taken me. My heart felt sad and heavy, as it quite often did when I was in a bad place. The odd thing, though, was that my jaw had started to ache early in the morning, but by lunchtime the whole of my jawbone was feeling solid and vulnerable, and I was feeling positively strange. The routine was that I would spend the rest of the afternoon at Nigel's mum and dad's house; then Nigel would come to their house after he finished work. We'd all have tea together, then we would go home. Only this day the routine was not working out as expected. I tried to control my emotions, but both mum and dad knew me very well. They were aware that I wasn't normal. I was subdued, quiet and didn't want any lunch, the usual symptoms, but it wasn't until around 1.30pm that they realised to what extent. I was beginning to panic, the lunchtime news was on. I couldn't understand what was happening to me. I made a decisive move off the settee where I had been laying. Mum and dad were sat in their usual armchairs.

Dad put his pipe down in the ashtray and said, 'What's the matter, duck?' Dad always had a calming effect over me. Apart from loving him as a real dad, I had great respect for him and I knew I could always turn to him for advice. He was calm in a crisis, one of the many traits that Nigel had inherited.

'My jaw feels funny, it feels like it's going to lock,' I mumbled in panic mode.

By now mum was sat in an upright position on the edge of her chair with a confused expression on her face. 'Look, pet, I think we'd better ring the doctor for some advice.'

'Mmm, please mum, I don't like it, it's frightening me,' I said.

The only advice the surgery could give was to 'contact Charles Clifford, the dental hospital.' They took some details and background information on my recent illness, and suggested we drive down to see them asap. I'd never been in the building before. Neither had Nigel's mum and dad. In fact, it wasn't an easy place to find, what with all the new one-way street restrictions being put in place. By now I was in no fit state to try to help navigate. I'd gone into trance mode, which was how Nigel used to describe my demeanour when this happened. The room was packed full of miserable-looking people, me included. Obviously, we were all in the same situation, all in pain! Mum sat holding my hand on one side of me and dad on the other. I cushioned my head on mum's shoulder and sat patiently, waiting for my turn.

Eighty minutes later my name was called. 'Alright, pet,' mum said, turning to me. 'Come on, they've called us'. My speech was slurred and I felt tired and drunk. I was escorted into a large black dentist chair, which I flopped into. It reminded me of a similar black chair way back in my childhood. A large window was directly in front of me. All I could see was the sky, as a large gentleman reclined my chair backwards. I was finding it increasingly difficult to speak, let alone make sense. It was all quite surreal. I felt as though I'd been in that chair an age, but obviously my recollection was somewhat tainted. All I can remember is the pain and discomfort that the instruments caused as they probed my mouth. The dental nurse who was holding my hand gave me a reassuring smile, as she must have seen the tear that was creeping into the corner of my eye. Mum squeezed my arm, smiled and whispered, 'Be brave, pet.' But by now the tear had escaped and was trickling down my face.

Lockjaw

I'd heard of it, but I didn't know of anybody who'd experienced it!

Anyway, it didn't matter now as I could give a first-hand account. As I lay prostrate in the chair I felt as though I was having an out of body experience. I stared skywards. Allowing the scenario to be played out around me, I was conscious but I didn't feel it. Stuff was happening around me, I could hear it, but in my mind's eye I'd clocked out.

The edges were becoming blurred. I can remember feeling drunk and dizzy, warm and cosy, but very sleepy yet almost comfortable in my own bubble of existence. I wanted to close my eyes and go to sleep. The past ten months had been incredibly difficult. What must I have done in a former life to deserve this? It must have been a bad thing. I didn't understand back then, but OCD was raising its ugly head again. It just couldn't resist the opportunity to hurt me. Oh no, please, go away, please! The next thing I can remember was the pain returning and a crack. I was no longer tired, but the jaw was back in place... or so they all thought. The pain returned with a vengeance.

I must have been in a state of shock, because I can't really remember getting out of the chair, or even travelling back to Nigel's mum and dad's in the car. What I do remember was thinking: this is still not right, it's not sorted. Nigel had been made aware of the afternoon's events via mum and a phone call, so that evening he arrived home relatively early. 'Now then,' he said, 'I can't leave you alone for two minutes, can I?' I must have had such a vacant expression on my face, because Nigel cupped my face in his hands as he knelt down and said, 'It's okay, honey bun, that's over now.' My eyes sprung a leak again as tears silently dripped onto my jumper. How could I tell him that I didn't think that was the case? All I could do was to hope that I was wrong. But I was not wrong.

We arrived home at around 8.15pm. Bassett is only a five minute drive away from Nigel's mum and dad's. I'm pretty vague about most of what happened next, but what I do remember is Nigel encouraging me to get undressed and climb into bed.

I felt weird, my mouth and jaw ached terribly, yet I was just wandering around in total oblivion, almost trance-like. Nigel sat me on the edge of the bed, undressed me and got me into my pyjamas. As he pulled the covers back he said gently, 'Elaine, come on, get in.'

I always know when Nigel is getting cross or frustrated with me, because he uses my 'Sunday name': Elaine. This was one of those occasions. He helped me into bed, got undressed and proceeded into the bathroom. I lay in bed, gazing at the bedroom ceiling. Something was happening with my jaw and I couldn't control it. I tried to call out to Nigel, but my mouth wouldn't work. I was feeling distant again, like earlier in the afternoon, but much more so. I felt my chin and realised that the wetness was saliva dribbling out of the corners of my mouth, but I had no control over it. Tears streamed down my face, but I was unable to call for help. My chest was tight and I was becoming short of breath. I didn't realise at the time how close I was to permanent sleep. I was very tired again, but I wasn't warm like earlier. I didn't understand what was happening. I was frightened and just wanted to see Nigel's face again. It can only have been a matter of minutes, but it seemed much longer, when Nigel's face came into view as he leaned over me and started to shake me. To be perfectly honest, I'm unable to be articulate enough to describe the exact sequence of events that took place over the next few hours. All I do remember is the fear I saw in Nigel's eyes as he struggled to make sense of what was happening.

I was told days later that what actually happened is that I dislocated my jaw. This was caused due to an allergic reaction to some new drugs that I had recently had prescribed for my condition. The life-threatening situation, that took place that evening, was that the drugs had caused such a violent reaction that the outcome culminated in me swallowing my tongue, and it was only due to Nigel's quick thinking and actions that night that I am here today to tell my story.

Apparently, Nigel dialled 999 to the emergency services, and immediately he was connected to an online paramedic who guided him through the delicate operation of retrieving my tongue from my throat, ultimately securing my survival. Nigel was told that a paramedic team was on their way to us, but that until they arrived Nigel had to remain calm and listen carefully to what he had to do. She told him that she would stay talking to him until the paramedics arrived, but that he had to do what she said, to help me until they did. Even now, sixteen years on, Nigel still finds that time very difficult to talk about and discuss. At the time of writing this chapter we are on a condor ferry from Poole, accompanied by our little Chihuahua (Chico). We are just approaching Jersey where our pride and joy sits in Elizabeth Marina, our boat 'Black Pearl'. The date is 22nd May 2013. It has been with some reluctance that Nigel has only now agreed to describe to me in detail the events of that night for the sake of me writing my book.

Learning Curve

Perhaps it's similar to how you feel when you bring a child into this world. I certainly felt a massive responsibility towards Marty and Georgie. They needed me and I definitely needed them. I needed them for my sanity and well-being.

Over the weeks and months that followed, an incredible bond between two animals and a human was forged. Throughout my chemo and radiotherapy they were always there for me, it was as though they knew I needed them. After each treatment they would be stood next to the gate at the top of our paddock to greet me when I stepped out of the car. They would strain their necks, humming, waiting for me to wander over to them both for a stroke and cuddle. I would say out loud, 'good boys, guys, waiting for mum again,' as I nuzzled my head between them, putting an arm around their necks and pulling them towards me. Marty, being the cheeky one, would give a little snort and jump sideways when he got excited, which tended to be quite often. He craved love and affection, and I happily gave it in abundance. As I had expected, the treatment was quite unpleasant at times but nevertheless, no matter how bad I felt, I could always wander out into the paddock and, when I saw Marty and Georgie waiting for me, they always managed to make me smile.

The more time I spent with Marty and Georgie, the more I came besotted with them. They were rapidly getting under my skin, and I found I could while away hours just watching them. They fascinated me like no other animal had managed to do so in the past. I loved the way they interacted with each other. At sunset they would follow each other, dancing. 'Pronking' is actually what their dancing is called, and it's so funny to watch. Their legs almost look like pogo sticks, and they spring on all four legs high in the air, land, and off they go again in a rhythmic-like fashion. In all the text books they say if alpacas and llamas are seen pronking, it's because they are happy and settled. On a regular basis Marty and Georgie would go through this little ritual, and I can't explain just how warm this made my heart feel. I could sense that maybe, just maybe, my time was coming, my time to be a more content and happy person; my time to find that true happiness which had eluded me throughout so many years of OCD.

During the autumn my chemo and radiotherapy was coming to an end, and I began to think how great it would be to add a couple of females to my little herd. I was surprised at how well Nigel accepted my cautious idea. Looking back, maybe he was expecting it! Two weeks later we were travelling down to Reading again to take a look at females. It was as easy as that. We'd decided that we would go back to the breeder who we had bought Georgie from. I got on with Joy (the breeder) and I was impressed with her stock and the way she dealt with them, so it made sense to pay her another visit. When we arrived, a pen of females had been rounded up for us to cast our eye over and, although I was very much still a novice where alpacas were concerned, I knew what I liked the look of. I was surprised to find out that the group of alpacas I had picked out as 'favourites' were in fact the top quality that Joy had on the farm at that time. In layman's terms, top quality is defined by: fineness of fibre, density, crimp, lustre, handle and overall micron count. In general terms, the lower the micron count the higher quality the fibre usually is. There are many more requirements that quantify top quality, for instance conformation is extremely important. For breeding animals we look for straightness of legs, front and back, a nice compact body, a good head with neat spear-shaped ears, a good bite (if the lower or upper jaw is undershot or overshot, that is not a good bite) and a good tail set. The requirements list goes on.

My ultimate aim has always been to strive to improve the alpaca industry in the UK, and breed from only the finest animals I can. There is absolutely no point at all in breeding from inferior animals. It's not fair on the animals, and I firmly believe that it's just not the ethical thing to do. We need to have a very critical eye for the animals we choose to breed from. I strongly believe that, as breeders, we have a responsibility to the breed, and our decisions should always be based on this premise and not just on monetary gain.

Joy was very gracious with her comments on my choice of animals, and was complimentary in pointing out that I had 'a good eye for an alpaca'.

After several long hours I had finally chosen my first two females, Sophia and Carla. In addition we had made the decision to purchase a young, but promising, ten month old male called Bomber, in the hope that 18 months on he would be working as a stud male servicing the two girls. With the benefit of hindsight, I wouldn't advise the extra outlay in cost today in buying a stud male. There are so many excellent studs in the UK today that you might as well take your pick, instead of burdening your small herd with just one stud of your own. You can very quickly find yourself in a mess with genetics. These days many breeders provide an on-site breeding service or what we call a 'drive-by mating', where a stud is brought to your premises to do the deed, then immediately taken back home in the trailer.

We had driven down in Nigel's short wheelbase, silver Shogun, so we were not in a position to take the animals home that same day. We arranged with Joy that we would make the journey down again the following week, when we could collect all three alpacas together. Just one small problem. We didn't own a trailer!

The conversation on the way home was interesting, as I don't think Nigel had anticipated signing on the dotted line that day! Neither do I think he realised just how these three alpacas were about to change our lives for ever! This was just another chapter in our ever-changing life!

Then there were Five

'I love my work' Sneaking a kiss with Alya

The following week we made the same journey down to Oxfordshire, but this time we had a trailer in tow. We were fortunate that Brian and Mary, who lived in the farm next door, had very kindly said that we could borrow their trailer. It towed really smoothly on the back of the Shogun, and I was surprised when Nigel passed a comment saying, 'Perhaps we might need to invest in one of these.'

I said nothing but thought, 'Mmm, that sounds interesting.'

All three animals loaded well and, after saying our goodbyes, we were back on the motorway, destination Sheffield.

It was still daylight when we reached home, mums and dads where waiting for us to watch the unloading procedure, just as they had done several months earlier. It was just as exciting and didn't disappoint, only this time it was really amusing watching the eager faces of Marty and Georgie, stepping sideways, to get a better glimpse of what was about to come out of the large silver box which had been driven into their paddock; the large silver box more commonly known to us as a 'stock trailer'. Their little faces were a joy to watch; hums of all different pitches were emanating from them.

It was just like watching excited children anticipating opening their presents on Christmas morning. We'd separated our paddock into two. Marty and Georgie were in the far one, so that we could drive straight into the paddock to unload the girls and Bomber. At ten months old, Bomber was not physically able to cover or hassle the girls so, for the first few days, I thought it best for him to run him with them. That way he could get associated with Marty and Georgie over the fence that separated them, rather than trying to integrate him straight away.

I was a little worried that my boys may try to bully him, seeing as he was a newcomer and younger but, to be honest, that concern was totally unfounded. When I finally did integrate him a few days later, he made friends with Georgie immediately and it was Marty who was the one that was a bit stand-offish.

As Nigel unlocked the back of the trailer, I glanced over to mums and dads who looked as excited as I did. They'd given me so much love and support throughout that I wanted to share this experience with them. Sophia was the first one to place a foot on the trailer ramp, closely followed by Carla, and even closer by Bomber. The boys on the other side of the fence could hardly contain their excitement. The smell of girls had obviously reached their nostrils, and they were keen to see more and investigate further. The girls wandered towards the boys in a nonchalant manner, casually teasing the two boys as they hesitated at the side of them. When females are open (not pregnant) they give off a scent to males, who instantly pick up the signal that they are ready to breed; therefore, as with all males (humans included), this heightens their excitement to the point where male alpacas produce a vocal noise called orgling (oh yes, this is fact). When a young male is ready to start working, which is usually around three years of age, we sometimes need the assistance of an experienced stud male to show the young male the art of seduction!

By running the youngster alongside the stud, he picks up the basics of sex education ('This is how it's done, son!') He will learn his trade by watching and listening to the stud's vocal tones, which he in turn will then try to copy and perfect.

As with owning any animal, there is an enormous amount of fulfilment and enjoyment to be had, and I had been soaking up every bit of that. I had fallen head over heels in love with these animals and it was fantastic! That's why it hit me so hard. One spring day Nigel, me and both dads were busy in the paddock. It was one of those warm April days that gives you a taster of what's to come. The birds were singing, the air was warm and life was pretty good. Nigel's mum had just shouted, 'Coffee in ten minutes,' out of the open kitchen window, when I was startled to hear my dad's voice shout, 'Get off, ya daft bugger!'

Marty, my llama, was on his back legs with his front legs over dad's shoulders!

If I hadn't have been so worried it would have looked really comical.

'Lol,' Nigel shouted, at the same time as I was running towards dad shouting, 'Marty, Marty.'

Luckily dad was fine, albeit a little bit shaken. Marty was a huge llama, standing around 6ft on all fours, so he dwarfed dad when he was stood on his back legs.

I was alarmed, because this was so out of character. Marty had never shown any sort of aggression before and, in actual fact, we had created such a bond that he would allow me to rest my head on his back whilst laid on the grass. He would just sit in a cushed position (all four legs tucked under his body), very contented, and he seemed as relaxed with me as I was with him. 'Surely this was not a show of aggression,' I thought, 'but merely an act of over-exuberance on Marty's part.'

Nigel wasn't convinced, and we had many conversations as to why this could have happened. I tried to convince myself that this unfortunate display was just a one-off, just a hiccup, but I couldn't get a niggling doubt out of my head that I could well have caused this problem. As we loaded Marty into the trailer, Ordell's last words to me were, 'Dear Elaine, enjoy him, have lots of fun with him, but remember he's a llama; treat him as one.' Twelve months later, little did I know that those words would come back to haunt me.

Painful Goodbyes

It was an awful few weeks. Marty's behaviour had worsened. In desperation I put a call through to Ordell for help. The conversation was pretty much as I expected it. We talked through the sequence of events that had taken place over the previous few weeks, the problems that come with being too hands-on with an animal that can imprint on a human. I'm talking about BMS (Berserk Male Syndrome), as it's more commonly known. BMS is a syndrome that can occur in young male llamas/alpacas when an over-indulgence of human handling has taken place with an animal in its infancy. Sometimes as alpaca/llama breeders we have no choice but to be hands-on with a young male animal for the animal's survival. For instance, if a dam (pregnant female alpaca) was to lose her life during parturition, then it would be necessary to step in to bottle-feed the cria; otherwise it would be certain death for the cria. Sometimes an orphan cria can be adopted by another female but, if not, then it is left to us as breeders to be that surrogate mother. Believe me, it's not easy; I've done it on several occasions, and it certainly comes with a great deal of heartache. Some I win, but some I lose. Call it luck or skill, but I've been fortunate to have more successes than failures. I must admit to getting an incredible feeling of satisfaction when I see a young cria, a few weeks on from fighting for its life, skipping around the paddock with its own kind. To know that I have played a major role in saving a cria's life gives me immense pleasure and pride.

The outcome of our discussions was that, in Ordell's opinion, the only option we had was to geld Marty as soon as possible, although it was still not a forgone conclusion that it would work. Marty was sixteen months old by now and his hormones had already started to kick in. It was possible that we were trying to lock the door after the horse had already bolted, so to speak. It was my last resort though, so I had to go with it. In the end I made the decision to have both Marty and Georgie gelded at the same time. Georgie never had been breeding quality so it made sense. When the day came it proved quite problematic. Marty, being a llama, was much heavier than Georgie and, although he was becoming increasingly difficult with other people, he was always calm around me. The problem we had was getting him sedated sufficiently to complete the mini op. Alpacas were still pretty rare in the UK, so most vets didn't have much experience in handling or treating them; so it was a little bit of a trial and error. Even now, sixteen years on, there are still no vaccines that are licensed for alpacas/llamas. Eventually, after increasing the dose of sedation, it started to take effect and I could feel his weight slowly sliding down my body, until he was laid partly on my lap and partly on the field shelter floor. He looked so content and sleepy as I stroked his face, his long eyelashes blinked as he stared at my face for reassurance. 'Good boy, my beauty'.

I whispered, 'Good boy, go sleeps, mummy's here.' As I gazed into his eyes, I couldn't help but feel so sad and guilty. I knew then that I'd caused this; it was of my doing and I felt so bad. Because of my vulnerability, state of mind, insecurities or whatever I'd been too needy of him. I still believe to this day that he connected with me in some unique way and he understood and recognised that I was in a bad place. I craved his love and affection and he gave it back so unreservedly. To be understood and wanted by an animal is one of the best feelings I have ever experienced in my life, and one that I continue to experience. I feel very privileged to be accepted into their world, and that's something I will never take for granted.

Four weeks on and there was still no improvement with Marty's behaviour. I didn't expect instant results, but I hoped that a change would be imminent. There was none. In fact, the situation worsened if anything. Up until now Marty had been tolerant of Nigel in the paddock when I was around, although Nigel never really pushed his luck too much when he was alone. Even this didn't last though. Marty had begun to see me as his property and it was his job, not only to protect me, but to own me.

Unfortunately, the day came when Marty played his joker card once too many times, even with Nigel. I was heartbroken. We were in the paddock. Nigel had merely put his arm around my shoulder, when he was taken off his feet and catapulted several feet across the paddock like a rag doll. I was horrified with what I had just witnessed. My Marty: why, why had he done that when all Nigel had ever shown him was kindness? The following week was a difficult one, as Nigel had put his foot down and said enough was enough.

Nigel put a call through to Ordell to discuss the dilemma we now found ourselves in. As a last resort, Ordell gave Nigel the contact details of a couple of people in Northampton who dealt with problem llamas. Mary and David Pryse ran a trekking centre with llamas, but they had been known to help people with difficult llamas, having numerous and successful outcomes. We had no other ideas, so Nigel put a call through to them and, after a little bit of persuasion, they reluctantly agreed to come up to meet Marty. Two days later, Mary and David arrived at Bassett. That same morning I'd sat on the grass beside Marty with my arm around him and talked to him as I so often did, only this time it was not a conversation that I ever thought would take place. He seemed to sense my uneasiness. Holding back the tears was impossible and, in fact, I let them flow freely. Some people might think I'm crazy but, to be honest, I'm not really bothered what they think, this animal understood me and I understood him; the bond between us was incredible and I needed to explain to him how I felt. I talked and he listened, apart from the occasional hum.

I was sobbing uncontrollably as the door on the trailer was closed with Marty inside. His head was still just visible and the oh-so-familiar hum ripped my heart apart. David and Mary had agreed to work with him for six months. Three months into the six was when the phone call came; Marty's aggression had worsened. David, although quite a burly chap, had been injured by Marty, and they had decided enough was enough. We were told that they were with him when he was put to sleep. He was calm and relaxed. I prayed his last thoughts of me were of all the incredible times we'd shared together in his oh-so-short life. I also prayed for his forgiveness.

Horsey Encounters

I'd always loved horses. My uncle Stan had first introduced me to them. He had a few horses on his farm, one of which was a little Shetland pony I'd named 'Toggles'. Toggles ran together with a few stallions in the top field. He was a grey roan and, although he was by far the smallest in the field, he'd definitely not realised. He was a little pony with a massive character, very feisty and certainly top of the pecking order. He would often double-barrel the stallions if they got too close but, the funny thing was, they allowed him to get away with it. I never had any formal training or lessons to be taught how to ride, apart from Uncle Stan throwing me on Toggles' back, no saddle, no bridle, just a head collar and lead rope attached. Back in those days it was just a case of learning as I went along. The BHS (British Horse Society) would have had a fit if they had seen me. I never wore a riding hat because I didn't own one! No fancy jodhpurs or riding boots, instead just a pair of old wellies and trackie bottoms. Having said that, I certainly developed a good seat, as we say in the trade; basically, in layman's terms, it means developing the technique of how to stay on the back of a horse without falling off! Wow, did I have to learn quickly.

Looking back, I suppose my confidence and husbandry skills, since owning my alpacas, had made me blossom as a person, and I began thinking of trying my hand at other things. My childhood days were long gone, but my love of horses had never waned. As a little girl I used to daydream about one day owning my own horse. I never really believed that it would happen though: ... until now! It was August 1999 and I had been having riding lessons for several months at our local riding centre, Smeltings Farm. Vicki and Mike Stenton owned the establishment, and played a very hands-on role with the day-to-day running of the centre/ livery yard. Alongside them worked both their sons, Damian and

Mark, so all in all it was quite a family affair. Since my diagnosis, followed by all the treatment, Nigel tried to give me virtually anything I wanted; he would have given me the moon if it would have been possible. As usual on a Saturday morning, we were sat outside in the garden with mums and dads drinking coffee. It was a beautiful sunny day and Nigel was glancing through the Yorkshire Post newspaper. The Yorkshire Post was renowned for being very farm orientated, with articles and advertisements for the buying and selling of farming machinery and such like. All different sorts of animals were advertised for sale, from domestic cats and dogs through to commercial sheep, cattle, pigs, goats, poultry and horses.

'Elaine, what about a horse?' said Nigel, as he peered over the top of the newspaper.

'What about a horse?' I questioned back.

'Well, we've got a stable doing nothing. Why don't I buy one for you? We are paying for riding lessons, so it makes sense to get one of our own.'

'Nigel,' I exclaimed, 'I haven't got the experience to own a horse, never mind look after one!'

'Why not?' he said. 'You can learn'. He leaned across me, placing the newspaper on my knees. 'Look, there's loads for sale, have a look through and see if you like the sound of any, and we can go and have a look'.

'What, just like that?' I laughed.

'Yeah, exactly like that,' he smiled back.

That's one thing that I've always admired about Nigel; I've never known him deterred by anything or anybody. In Nigel's eyes, there is nothing that is unachievable if you want it badly enough. The problem was that it would be me doing the riding and the looking after of this horse, and I wasn't quite as confident as Nigel was that it would be as easy as he thought. However, I was very excited at the prospect of possibly making a childhood dream come true, so I read on with interest. The seed had been planted, and it wasn't long before I had picked out a handful of horses that I liked the sound of.

'Give 'em a call, then. Tomorrow's Sunday. Let's spend the day looking for a horse. We can do two or three viewings, I would have thought, if we plan a round trip.'

'Nigel,' I said, 'you make it sound like we're looking for a new house, not a horse.'

'Well, there's plenty for sale,' he said. 'We want to buy, people want to sell, so it sounds pretty straightforward to me.'

That's how Nigel sees life. Make a decision; go and do it. Failure never enters his head, nothing is impossible.

I threw my hands up in the air and wandered inside to make the calls. I wished I had a quarter of the confidence that Nigel had.

The next morning I must admit to being really excited. I'd not slept that soundly due to my excitement. I knew now that I was going to own my own horse in the near future, and my tummy was doing cartwheels! I'd made several calls the previous day to a few horse owners who were advertising their horses for sale. A couple of these were horse dealers, but some were private sellers. Nigel had decided on our first destination and our last port of call, so we had a plan to work to. We didn't have sat-nav then, so it was down to my map reading capabilities to get us to our venues, without taking too many wrong turns. Unfortunately, map reading was not one of my better skills back then, so there were quite a few gasps from Nigel of, 'Oh no, Elaine, not again!' I could have done with a tape recorder to switch on, the amount of times I went wrong saying, 'Sorry, love.'

However, despite my little hiccups, we did manage to arrive at every destination, give or take an hour or two late. I rode every horse that we went to see, but nothing I saw was really what I was looking for. They were nice horses, but I just wasn't bowled over by any. For me, buying a horse was a big decision. It wasn't like buying an item of jewellery that you could take back to the shop for a refund if you changed your mind. No, it was much more than that, and I had to be as sure as sure I could be that it was the right type of horse for me. I was totally inexperienced, green, as we would say in the horse world. In hindsight, as I would find out soon enough, we should really have enrolled the help of someone like Vicky Stenton, who had years and years of horsey experience, to guide and advise us on what we should be looking for. But we didn't. Actually, I didn't really know anyone well enough to feel comfortable asking. It was early days in the building of friendships in the horsey world, so we just carried on regardless. Every opportunity we had was taken up searching for horses that sounded like they would suit, not just at weekends. Sometimes, Nigel finished work early and we would set off north or south wherever the horse was based.

It's funny, but after a while I found it quite frustrating not being able to find what I wanted. To be honest, I didn't have any firm requirements, probably because I was so green. I wasn't even bothered what breed, type or colour I wanted, and that really does show how green I was! Thinking back, it was a recipe for disaster before I even started. Since then I've come along way in the horsey world and learned a great deal. I've had to. You could say I threw myself in at the deep end; it was either sink or swim and I didn't want to sink! I'd had enough of that over the previous years. I was determined I was going to swim! We've laughed about it since, but there was one occasion in particular that will stick in my mind whilst searching for my perfect mount. I had never considered a mare (adult female), it was always a gelding (castrated male). I'd mainly ridden geldings at Smeltings, and mares were renowned for being a bit temperamental (for any men reading this do NOT comment!) Anyway, there was this one mare that I'd come across, which sounded interesting. It was on a livery yard. I'd not spoken to the owner of the yard, but I had spoken to the head girl. She had said the mare was certainly worth a look and a ride, as she wasn't 'mare-ish' at all (horsy term).

Not true, as I was to find out at my peril. The ménage was in use for teaching, so we were taken into a large field adjacent to the ménage. What happened next is not for the faint-hearted. Nigel had recently bought a video camera and was enjoying trying it out with me on horseback. I was in agreement with him filming, as I thought it would be useful for me to see my riding position. 'Mmm, she does seem quite laid back, this mare,' I thought. 'Maybe she's a possibility after all'. Not so, as I was shortly to find out. The head girl said the mare was already warmed up as she'd been used in a lesson, so no need for me to do much stretching with her. I set off in walk down the long side of the field, putting her into trot soon after. I was surprised how quickly she responded to my leg aids - we were off in no uncertain terms. Meanwhile, Nigel had set the camera rolling. He said later that as we trotted off down the field he thought, 'Wow, Elaine's certainly putting this one through its paces.' Wrong again! It was the mare that was putting me through my paces. I tried to stay calm and keep relaxed, but by now the mare had voluntarily gone into canter, and I was beginning to feel tense. I was reacting just like they say in the text-books you shouldn't do. By now I was trying to decide how best to stop the bloody thing. The mare's pace and speed were increasing. Back at the other end of the field, Nigel was still unaware of my plight. He says he remembers thinking how confident I must have felt to be upping the pace so soon. Wrong again! In fact he said it wasn't until the mare started galloping that he started to panic as he realised that I was struggling to keep control. Nigel stopped filming and turned towards the head girl, who was by now trying to muffle her sniggers with her hand. She obviously thought it was amusing, watching what must have looked like a scene out of a comedy sketch being played out before her. The funny thing was that although Nigel was no longer filming, the camera was still rolling and in his panic he dropped the camera, which was still busy filming the scenery. We have laughed about this so many times since, but I can tell you it was no laughing matter at the time. Nigel's shaky voice could be heard shouting at the head girl to help me, and the camera was still merrily filming various varieties of grasses, whilst being kicked around the field in earnest. Thinking about it we could have sent that clip to 'You've been framed'. I'm sure we could have got £200 for it!

All's well that ends well and no lasting damage was done, apart from my pride.

I did get the mare to stop eventually, by turning her into a tight circle whilst still in full flight. She didn't like that, but by this time I wasn't too concerned about how she felt. We came to an abrupt halt, with me still in shock at the whole episode. Nigel was running over to me as I slithered off the saddle into his arms, looking rather dishevelled. My legs felt like jelly as they hit the ground, and I was relieved that Nigel was there to keep me vertical. What an initiation ceremony for my first major horsey encounter. I was not in a rush to repeat it! We still laugh about it now, and I can't really blame the head girl for finding it funny so, wherever you are, head girl, I forgive you.

Merit, alias Danny

'Merit' my first horse

After several weeks of searching for my new mount, I was convinced that I had spoken to the owner of a horse I thought sounded perfect. I felt I'd asked all the right questions and, funnily enough, I'd had just the right answers! The arrangements were made, and Sunday morning we set off to East Yorkshire, destination Beverley. We arrived early. I had been told another prospective customer was due that day, so I was keen to arrive first, hoping that I would be given first refusal if we decided to buy him. The horse was called Danny and the lady was a private seller. I felt better about that, as I'd been warned that dealers could be a bit dodgy. First impressions, and I was impressed. He was an Appaloosa cross, but strangely enough he didn't look like one. That didn't strike me as odd at the time, though. Danny was chestnut in colour, fifteen hands and two inches tall, with one white sock and a blaze down his head. He looked very smart and I couldn't wait to get on him. Nicky, the owner, tacked him up and led him out into a ménage. 'Okay, he's all yours,' she said, as she walked him up to the mounting block.

Climbing on board was my very first mistake! No experienced horsewoman would ever ride a horse that they had never seen being ridden by the owner before mounting themselves. In fact, she never did ride him whilst we were there. However, he seemed great and I walked him, trotted him and even popped him into canter a little. I was smitten. A younger girl arrived at the ménage. Nicky introduced me, and asked if I would like to try Danny out on a hack, accompanied by the younger girl. Crikey, these people were falling over themselves to accommodate me, how nice was that? How naive was that? Second mistake: my heart was ruling my head! The truth was that I always try to see the best in people, and I hope to be treated that way by others. Sadly, this is not always the case, as I have learned over the years. The alarm bells still didn't start ringing when a pheasant flew out of the hedgerow. Danny never spooked (horsey term), never batted an eyelid. Not the case for the other horse. He shot forward, startled by the pheasant, and the younger girl went out of the side door (horsey term for falling off sideways).

The times I think back to that day! Nicola must have been laughing all the way to the bank! Yes, you guessed, I bought him. I'd fallen for him hook, line and sinker!!!

The following week we were going away to Jersey for the week, so it was decided that we would take delivery of Danny on our return. Nicky had said that she would deliver him, so the date was agreed. I did enjoy our holiday in Jersey, but I was so excited about Danny's arrival that I couldn't think of anything else. The only thing I didn't like about Danny was his name. He just didn't look like a Danny and, personally, I thought it was a bit of a naff name for such a good looking horse. I decided I would call him Merit, don't ask me why, but it just suited him. Back then I didn't know that horsey superstitions say that it is bad luck to change a horse's name. Oh no, another mistake. They were mounting up quickly!

The day of Merit's arrival was here. I was surprised when Nicky pulled down the back of the horse box to see a pony tied up alongside Merit. Nicky assured me that it was fairly common practice to travel a horse with a field buddy, if one of the horses was a little nervous travelling alone. Yet again, I took her word for it and thought no more of it. It never occurred to me that the pony travelling back would be alone!

All horses are herd animals and prefer to have company rather than be alone. I had explained that his friends in the field adjacent would be an alpaca and a llama, but she had said, 'Oh well, at least he's got some company.' Whilst Nicky ran through feeds and other stuff with me, both Merit and pony friend were grazing happily. All seemed well until Nicky started to load the pony back into the horse box. Merit started whinnying to his friend, who in turn was whinnying back to Merit, sounding equally distressed. 'Once we're on the road and out of sight, he'll settle,' she called across to me. 'Are you sure?' I questioned, not at all sure he would.

'Yes, definitely, just give him a day or two'. By now Nicky had closed the back of the horse box, and Merit began galloping up and down the fence line. I thought, at one stage, that he might try and jump the paddock gates, but thankfully he didn't. Nicky jumped in the cab, started the engine and set off down the lane on her way back to Beverley. Suddenly I felt alone, just like I had when we arrived home with Marty and Georgie eighteen months earlier. I felt sorry for Merit too; he must have felt terribly alone. He'd been brought to a place he didn't know, a new owner he didn't know but, worst of all for him, he'd had his best friend taken away before his eyes. I had so little experience back then, so I didn't realise how traumatic it must have been for Merit. Unfortunately, from this day on for Merit and me, the situation just got worse. We just didn't gel and we were on a downward spiral. I had read a lot and was still having riding lessons at Smeltings Riding Centre, but I know now all too well that experience and time around horses cannot be replaced with theory. The ingredients I had put into the mixing bowl were in the wrong order, the method would never work, and it was a recipe for disaster from start to finish.

I tried to hack him out on several occasions, but I had close shaves every time. I had managed to hack Merit down to Smeltings for a lesson or two, but even that wasn't easy. We'd shoot off at breakneck speed; then he'd stop suddenly, turn around on the spot, and we were off back to where we'd come from. I know reading about it now may sound amusing, but at the time it was really quite wearing. I think it seemed worse because I didn't really know anybody well enough in the horsey world to be able to turn to for advice. To be honest, it was just too much, too soon. One evening Nigel was trying to hold Merit whilst I was trying to mount him. I managed to get on, but as soon as I was in the saddle he reared. I was sure he was going over backwards and, to this day, I don't know how I stayed on. I'd owned Merit for just one day less than a fortnight when the inevitable happened.

It was a typical Saturday on a warm September day. That morning I'd been grooming Merit in the paddock. I thought a little time out together, without trying to put a saddle on his back, would do us both good. The warm sunshine looked like it was making Merit sleepy, and he looked so relaxed as I groomed his forelock and face with a small soft-bristled brush, so that I was finally beginning to think that we were getting somewhere. How wrong can one be? The next thing I was aware of was a searing pain in my chest. It all happened so quickly I didn't really grasp what was happening. My chest had been lunged at by Merit. The sheer force of Merit's jaw took my breath away, and for a few seconds he just wouldn't let go. I cried out Nigel's name, but he must have already been alerted by the commotion taking place. Merit had let go of me by the time Nigel arrived, but I was still fairly shocked by the whole incident. I couldn't believe what had just happened and why. 'For Gods sake,' said Nigel as he stared at my ripped T-shirt, 'what's happened?' I didn't know what I would find as I lifted my T-shirt to look at the damage, if any. Merit's teeth marks where clearly visible. Fortunately it was my cleavage that had taken the brunt of the bite. I was swollen and grazed but, thankfully, no worse than that. The next sensible step would have been to walk away from the situation. The trouble is, I don't always do 'sensible'.

Call it what you like, but I was upset, hurt and angry. I was determined to show Merit that I wasn't frightened or deterred by what had just happened. I certainly wasn't going to hit or harm him, but I intended to show him that he couldn't get the better of me. I tacked him up and climbed aboard. Nigel had been pleading with me not to ride him, but I wasn't really listening any more. Nigel and my dad were leaning over the fence at the top of the paddock, telling me to get off him. 'You've proved your point now, Elaine. Leave it now, call it a day'. 'Just once more round the paddock,' I said. Dad has never ridden horses in his life, but has worked with them in his younger days, so it came as no surprise when dad noticed that I hadn't actually asked Merit for canter. On the penultimate circle of the paddock, Merit had gone voluntarily in to canter. Normally, a horse will not change a gait unless they are asked to by the rider. The rider asks with a leg aid. 'One last circle and I'll call it a day,' I thought.

We turned in walk and headed downhill to the bottom of the paddock. Then it all went wrong. I've heard people explain their own personal experiences of accidents they've been involved in, and a comment that most people make is, 'Everything happened in slow motion.' Honestly, this is just so true. This is just how it felt for me. One second I was sat in the saddle and, the next thing I knew, I was being thrust upwards by the force of Merit bucking. He set off galloping horizontally across the paddock, and all I can remember thinking was, 'Shit, this is going to hurt!' We were approaching our post and rail fence rapidly, and I knew the outcome was not going to be good. Soon I was projected skyward, and heading through the air like superwoman. I actually remember thinking that whilst in full flight! On landing I didn't feel any pain, but I was mainly concerned about where Merit was, as I didn't want to be trampled by him.

I got to my knees, quickly turning around as I stumbled to my feet. Nigel and dad were running diagonally down the paddock towards me in panic mode, so I raised my arm above my head to wave 'slow down'. That's when I felt the pain. By the time dad and Nigel reached me, I was already walking back up the paddock, but I was rather preoccupied at trying to decide what had happened to my hand and wrist. They didn't look normal at all. Nigel was shaking his head at me as he stared at my hand. It wasn't good. After the initial rush of fear-fuelled adrenalin, my head was starting to spin and I felt decidedly sick. Dad and Nigel where supporting me under each shoulder when I said, 'I'm going.' My legs went to jelly and down I went. That's the last I can remember in any real detail until reaching the hospital, apart from occasionally opening my eyes on the journey to hear the car horn permanently being blown and my dad's voice saying, 'Nigel, speed cameras and police on here.'

Nigel was on a mission, and the mission was to get me to hospital on the shortest route possible and as quickly as possible. I think Nigel's motto was, if in dire straits blow your horn and to hell with the rest of the traffic!

On reaching the hospital, we were taken past all the other patients waiting their turn. After being examined by an A and E doctor, we were taken for an X-ray to find out the extent of my injuries. I'd broken my wrist in five places. They were nasty breaks and, because of this, they couldn't just set my arm in plaster. It would need surgery to be pinned. 'Bloody hell,' I thought, 'how long is this going to set me back for?' The only fortunate thing was, because of our private health insurance, I was able to be transferred to the good old faithful Thornbury Hospital yet again, instead of staying at the NHS Northern General. I'm not knocking our NHS at all. On the contrary, they do an absolutely fantastic job and we would be in a sorry state without them, but it seemed to make sense to transfer to Thornbury. After all, that's what we paid our premium for.

After ten days in hospital I got my release papers. My wrist had been pinned in five places, and I must admit to feeling a bit the worse for wear. Nevertheless, my main concern was not my wrist, but the horse that we'd got standing in our paddock at home. Where did we go from here? Luckily Vicki Stenton, who owned Smeltings Riding Centre, had heard about my accident, and the same night I arrived home, Nigel got a call from her. The decision was made between Nigel and Vicki that the best solution was that Merit should go to Smeltings for an intense six-week training livery, in the hope that Damian, Vicki's son and training manager, could re-educate him. That was the idea anyway. I didn't want to give up on Merit, and I wasn't about to throw the towel in that easily. That wasn't my way. I had to give Merit the benefit of the doubt.

Normality? Not a chance!

A proud moment taking first prize with Admiral

Every day of Merit's training I religiously went down to Smeltings to watch how he was coming along. He was making progress, but I was still a little concerned at how he would react with somebody on his back again. Although I respected Damian as a horseman, I was itching to see him ride Merit. I realised that he was trying to gain Merit's trust by working him from the ground, but at the same time I felt he needed to do that on his back. However, Damian was the expert so I decided to stay quiet and hoped Merit would come good. Four weeks into the six and I was getting frustrated; I felt it was time for me to get back on him. Damian tried to persuade me otherwise. I was still in plaster, but I'd made my decision - today was the day! 'Does Nigel know you're getting on board?' Damian asked, as he pulled the mounting block towards me. 'I'll be fine,' I answered, as I reached out for the reins and proceeded to put my left foot in the stirrup. My heart was beating twenty to the dozen, my mouth was dry, but I knew I had to relax. Merit would sense through my seat I was nervous, and that could be bad news for me. 'Sit like a sack of potatoes,' I kept thinking to myself, 'take deep breaths.' Actually, in the end, he never put a foot wrong, he was as good as gold and my optimism was renewed. If only he would have continued like that!

Towards the end of the six weeks, it was pretty obvious to me that Merit still needed a lot more work. I spoke to Vicki and Damian about my concerns but they were very non-committal. The training livery was expensive, and I just didn't see any point in throwing more money at it. To me there wasn't any considerable difference. The Smeltings' staff had been riding him in their staff lessons, which Damian normally taught, but he'd still thrown a couple of wobblys with them. These were people who had been brought up with horses all their lives. If Merit was still having tantrums with them on his back, I didn't think I had a cat in hell's chance. However, undeterred, I decided to continue to persevere with him. Around this time, I had been struggling with horrendous stomach pains. The pain was sometimes so bad I had difficulty in standing. One Saturday morning it all came to a head, but this time Nigel was around to witness it. I'd popped downstairs to our bedroom to collect a jacket from the wardrobe. We had planned to go to the local shops for a few bits and bobs, but never made it. The stomach pains returned, but this time they were so severe that they took my breath away. I couldn't help but panic. 'Jesus, what's happening?' I thought, as I dropped to my feet holding my stomach. It felt like somebody had just punched me in the stomach and winded me. In the background I could hear Nigel calling me from upstairs, 'Come on, bun, hurry up, let's get going.' Alarmed that I had not shouted back something sarcastic, he came to look for me. I was knelt down beside the open wardrobe door feeling sick with the pain. I couldn't catch my breath to speak to him, so instead just gripped his hand looking rather pathetic until the pain subsided.

Two days later we made the familiar journey back to Thornbury Hospital to see Mr Shorthouse. Nigel had put a call through to his private home on the Saturday, spoken to Tina, his wife, who we had got to know very well, and arranged an appointment for us to see Andrew on the Monday evening. Andrew (Mr Shorthouse, that is), gave me a thorough examination, as well as an internal examination and, although he couldn't feel anything suspicious, he suggested we see a gynaecologist whom he recommended. In fact, an appointment was made that night, and the following evening we visited a Mr T. C. Li in his consulting suites at his home in Psalter Lane. TC, as we used to refer to him, was a tiny little Chinese man. Everything was little about him. I can remember shaking his hand that first night and thinking how doll-like it was. I haven't got large hands, but they're still larger than TC's.

After nearly two hours with TC we knew that, from the pictures on the ultrasound scan, all was not well. We could see something that looked suspiciously like lumps around my ovaries. As TC moved the probe around I began to feel quite nauseous. Nigel was standing at the side of the examination table holding my left hand, and at the same time straining to determine what he was looking at on the screen. His pale face held all the same tension that I vividly remembered from three years before. 'Why us?' I thought, as a tear trickled down my left cheek, landing on the pillow that was supporting my head. All the experts say that if you get through the first five years without a re-occurrence of the cancer, then it's looking good. I was three years into my five.

Plans were made for me to be admitted to hospital as soon as possible. I'd asked TC if I could go onto Mappin Ward again, as I could at least take some comfort from knowing all the familiar faces of the staff. After all, Thornbury Hospital was unfortunately becoming home from home!

Within a few hours of the surgery, we had the results from TC. There were in fact three lumps removed. Only one had been seen on the scan, so the other two had either not been spotted or were growing at quite an alarming rate. I was now thirty-seven years of age and Nigel was forty-one and, although we had no children, we had not totally ruled out having any, up until being diagnosed with breast cancer. Once we'd had time to get our heads around the results we were faced with yet another major decision. TC told us, in no uncertain terms, that the safest option for me was to have a full hysterectomy although, on this occasion, the lumps were benign. Obviously that would be the end of any hope of children. Up until now I hadn't really been that bothered about children and neither had Nigel, but it's amazing how you feel when the option is taken away for ever. Nigel was immediate with his decision when he said to TC, 'There is no decision to be made for me. It's a no-brainer. I want Elaine to live and grow old with me.'

It was early December by now and Christmas was rapidly approaching. I wanted to have as normal a Christmas as possible, so the date for my hysterectomy was postponed until the 6th January 2000.

Principal Boy

My first competition with Prince in a hunter class

I'd been forced out of action for a while, what with all the recent surgery and recovery time. Twelve weeks was the norm for recovery, but I knew I wasn't about to spend that amount of time doing nothing. I had my alpacas, ducks, and geese to look after at home, and Merit on DIY Livery. When I was in plaster, I'd got around the problem of wheeling a barrow by tying a makeshift scarf around my neck as substitute for a handle; hence I could push a wheelbarrow with my right arm, along with my neck doing the work of my left arm: sorted. I needed to come up with a similar solution so I could get back on board Merit. I couldn't think of one, so in the end I thought, 'Sod it, just do it!'

Since owning Merit, I had never completed a hack. I'd only ever been in the ménage (which is a relatively safe arena), but my whole purpose of owning a horse was so that I could get pleasure in horse and rider being a partnership, spending enjoyable times together hacking round the countryside. I wasn't able to do any of this, because I kept being told by experienced people that Merit was 'far too unpredictable to take out on the road, it would be foolish to do so'.

This was beginning to frustrate the hell out of me, and I'd had enough. If Merit and I were not compatible then I wanted to find out sooner rather than later. If there was one thing that the cancer had taught me, that was that you only get one shot at life, you don't get a dress rehearsal, so just live life to the full; and that's exactly what I was going to do, one way or the other.

The outcome of my new-found confidence ended in disappointment on this occasion. I'd come to the end of the road with Merit. I decided that Merit and me should go out on a hack together, so I persuaded one of the other liveries to accompany me with their horse. What a nightmare; Merit was all over the place. At one point during the hack we ended up in someone's back garden. The house was a new build and the entire garden had been completely landscaped. We'd seen it being built over the previous few months as we passed it on our way home to Bassett. It didn't look landscaped when we'd finished with it. It looked more like a ploughed field waiting to be landscaped!!!

I was so embarrassed with the whole situation - what a disaster! We'd jumped into the horsey world with both feet first, and we were now paying for our impatience and inexperience. I didn't blame Merit though. In many ways I felt sorry for him. We were just the wrong combination at the wrong time. He was green, I was green, but we both needed to move on to pastures new (pardon the pun).

The following few weeks I put to good use. I spent a great deal of time at Smeltings farm learning my trade, as it were. Merit had been bought by Jason, one of the male staff at Smeltings who thought, 'Merit needed a man on his back,' and I was happy with the outcome. I was having three lessons a week, and had even progressed to jumping over small poles. I was feeling more and more confident as the weeks went by. I was riding a different horse each lesson, which was really good, as it gave me new experiences on how to handle different horses. I'd got the bit between my teeth now, and my thoughts turned towards looking to buy another horse. As with everything I do, I give it 100%. I'd read a lot and I learned a lot and I felt I was ready for the next step. On this occasion I was well prepared.

Every week Nigel's mum and dad took delivery of the Yorkshire Post newspaper, which they usually brought up to Bassett on Saturdays. It had an equestrian section, which advertised anything and everything equestrian as well as horses for sale. This week was the first week since selling Merit that I was keen to take a look. A colour photograph caught my eye, of a dapple grey horse with a beautiful outline. I was instantly drawn to it and read on eagerly. The advert finished with the caption, 'A real stamp of a horse.'

Three days later, we were on our way to York to take a look. The racing yard we were looking for was right next to York racecourse, and it looked very impressive as we approached down a long driveway. 'Enter through the main roller-shutter door, take a right turn and an immediate left, and Prince's stable is right at the end.' Those were the directions I'd written down from Ginny's mum on the phone two days previous. As we took the left turn I spotted a dapple grey horse tied up outside a stable. A teenager was grooming his mane, chatting away to an older lady.

'Wow,' I said, as I nudged Nigel, 'He looks fantastic.'

Just four days after visiting Prince for the first time we repeated the same journey. This time he would be returning home with us, and this time I knew it was right.

Ginny and her mum were very tearful as we loaded Prince into the horse trailer. We'd said our goodbyes, and promised to keep in touch, and wished each other well as we waved goodbye.

I'd secured a stable at Vicki's yard for Prince, and this time I felt I was on the right track - bring it on!

Although horses had been very much at the forefront of my mind and day-to-day life for the past few months, I still spent hours and hours in the paddocks at home with my other four-legged friends. They still fascinated me equally as much as when we first bought them. With each day, week and month that passed by I came to love them more than ever. I was experiencing a peace and tranquillity within my heart that I had never experienced before. The deep love and affection towards another human, be it a husband, parent or even friend, bears no comparisons or resemblance to that of an animal, and should not be mistaken for that. The two types of love are immensely different.

When I see on the television, or read in a newspaper the appalling atrocities that some humans can inflict on innocent animals, it makes me physically sick. In the supposedly civilised society we live in, there is no place for these evil, wicked humans. I am not a practising Christian (although I would say I have Christian beliefs), but on hearing such horrific acts of cruelty I could not and would not 'turn the other Cheek'.

Forty-two Empty Acres

With friends out on a hack. I dubbed us 'The Famous Five'

We were rapidly outgrowing our one-acre paddock at home, and I was beginning to get a little concerned about the amount of space we had for our little herd of alpacas. For guidance purposes, we usually say that six alpacas can be comfortably grazed on an acre. Our one acre paddock now had five alpacas grazing on it, but I'd already broached the subject with Nigel that I wanted to put Sophie and Carla into calf around Springtime 2001. Fifty weeks gestation period would mean that we would get our first two cria born in 2002, which was quite a way off, but I wanted to be organised and have sufficient grazing for all of them. Winters at Bassett can be harsh and severe and, at 1000ft above sea level, we get our fair share of snow. It's not unusual for us to experience temperatures as low as minus ten degrees Celsius. We've never actually been snowed in, but that's only because we have the farm machinery to dig our way out!

The spring/summer of 2000 turned out to be the beginning of a part of my life where I began to blossom in my own right. Nigel had been in business since the age of 17, and over the years we've been through the good times and the bad times that paddling your own canoe brings. I'd always been happy in a nine 'til five job. I liked routine, and working for the Sheffield Magistrates Court had given me that. I certainly wasn't the business material that was Nigel's forté. Prince and I were forming a good partnership; he was a real gem of a horse. He was forward going and could sometimes get quite excited, but I never felt frightened on his back, which was completely the opposite of how I felt with Merit.

My confidence was building all the time. I was learning quickly, and through Smeltings had met and palled up with a lady called Joy Cuthbertson. Joy was ten years my senior and I had been introduced to her via Vicki Stenton. I was still in pot from my accident on Merit, and Joy had just finished her riding lesson in the indoor school on her horse, Rupert. He was a Grey Connemara cross.

Joy had also been in a similar accident to mine a few years earlier, again after owning Rupert for just two weeks, so we immediately had something in common. We struck a chord with each other and became great friends. It was through Joy that I was encouraged to enter my first-ever competition with Prince. It was a hunter class taking place at our local riding club. The venue was only about one and a half miles from Smeltings, so we could easily hack down there and it would give the horses a good warm up. On the morning of the competition I was so nervous that I was permanently on the loo! Nigel had bought me a new competition jacket. It was black with a red silk lining and, together with my white shirt, black tie, beige jodhpurs, black boots and black velvet hat, 'I felt a million dollars'.

Nigel came down to the showground to watch Prince and me do our bit, and took loads of photos to remember the day by. My first initiation into the equestrian world of competition was deemed a success. I'd pushed myself to overcome my inhibitions and I was proud of that. By summertime I was riding Prince at least four or five times a week. I kept up with my regular lessons, but it was hacking out in the open countryside which I loved. Most of the time I would hack out in company, especially at the weekends, and our Saturday morning hack consisted of around five of us, which included Joy on Rupert, Barry on Colin, Clive on Tim, Wendy on Cassie and me on Prince. I dubbed us 'The Famous Five'. We had such laughs. Before we left the yard we'd all put our two penn'orth into which route we could take. I was always happy to go with the flow, as I was still learning all the different bridle paths but, more often than not, it would be Wendy and Clive that argued the toss. Most of the time Wendy would be the last one to stroll over to the mounting block, which used to irritate Clive immensely. We'd all be on board, our horses waiting patiently, and Wendy would be checking Cassie's bridle or stirrups muttering, 'We're not rushing, Cas, we're not rushing.' Clive would tut and look skywards cursing, 'She thinks we've got all day.' I must admit to finding the whole scenario amusing. We are fortunate that living in the countryside provides us with some fantastic bridle paths, and most of these are off-road and usually have some grassland, where we can get a good canter, or even a gallop if we're lucky. Barry owned Colin (I always thought it was a strange name for a horse), and invariably I used to call Colin: Barry, and Barry: Colin, much to the amusement of everybody else. However, Barry and myself were kindred spirits when it came to having fun on our horses. On most bridle paths, there are certain places where we normally agreed to have a canter. The horse and rider at the front checks to make sure everyone behind is ready, and then off we go in single file. On so many occasions, Barrie and myself would look across at each other, nod our heads and take flight, to the annoyance of everyone else. We loved racing each other equally as much as our horses did, side by side, backsides out of the saddle, we certainly went for it. We'd laugh out loud as we heard voices in the distance shouting, 'Slow down, slow down.' It was worth it, even though we would be berated by the others when they eventually caught us up!

It was towards the end of the summer that we got our first lucky break. Joy and I had ridden in the ménage that particular morning. We were going over our dressage test that we had to learn before the competition took place that weekend. As with most dressage competitions at our level, one was allowed to have a caller whenever a new direction and action was required. For example, at the letter C pick up trot in to a twenty metre circle, change the rein at B and walk. However, if you could memorise the test it was thought that you may be awarded higher marks, and you looked more polished as a partnership. We'd had a good morning session and so we thought we would reward ourselves with lunch in one of Hathersage's many coffee shops. It was whilst we were scanning the menu that I got a call through from Nigel. I quickly told Joy what I wanted to order and, like the good citizen I am, stepped outside to take the call. Nigel doesn't wear his heart on his sleeve, so sometimes it's difficult to tell if he's excited, especially when it's a phone conversation, but on this occasion the excitement in his voice was quite obvious.

'I've just had a very interesting conversation with the estate agents'.

The estate agents are local agents in Sheffield who sell private and commercial properties/land in and around the Sheffield area.

'Why? How come? What about?'

'Well, you know they're selling the sports ground by our factory'.

'Mmm, yeah,' I answered.

'They've just told me that a large chunk of land around the Ringinglow area is due to come on the market any time soon'.

'Never! Really? Whereabouts? How much is it?' The excitement was now getting to me. 'Oh, bun, this could be just what we're looking for!'

'Hang on, hang on, that's all they could tell me at this stage. Hopefully they'll be able to tell me more by the end of the week. It's still in the process of being finalised, so they can't tell me much more 'til then,' Nigel stressed.

I pressed the end button on my mobile as Joy was doing her best to attract my attention through the coffee shop window. 'Wow', I thought to myself, as I quickly re-entered the coffee shop. That evening we spent most of the night discussing the possibilities of whereabouts the land could be. The area in which we live is called 'The Mayfield Valley'. It is an area of outstanding natural beauty. It's also a green belt area, which means that the land is unable to be built on for residential purposes. 'Elaine, look, we'll just have to be patient and wait and see. It's impossible to guess where the land will be'. 'Yeah, I know, I know, but every bit of land that I know of is being grazed on around us; I just can't think where it can be,' I said, getting rather frustrated.

A few days later it was competition day: my first ever dressage test. This time the venue was at Far Nova Livery Yard. It was about a mile further than the Hallamshire Sports Ground where the hunter class had been held, so we had quite a way to hack this time. Again I was very nervous, but this time I'd got the added pressure of memorising the test routine. I'd been over and over it time and time again, but there was a lot to remember, and I was worried that, because I was so nervous, I might forget the test routine.

On arrival at the venue there were horses all over the place. The warm-up area was tiny, and I was relieved that we'd had quite a way to hack on the way down; at least our horses were well warmed up. After being allocated our slots, we were allowed to hover just outside the call-up area. Three horses were called up together and then each one individually was called into the arena. Joy was the one before me, which I was pleased about. They say owners are a bit like their horses; this is definitely true with Joy and Rupert. The minute Rupert stepped out of his comfort zone away from Prince he let out an almighty whinny and spun around to look for Prince. To Joy's embarrassment, a few muffled laughs were heard, which immediately cut the ice and settled my nerves. Actually they completed a clean routine with no hitches.

It was now my turn to face the music. 'Good Luck,' whispered Joy, as they passed me as they exited the arena and we entered. As we trotted in I patted Prince's neck and said quietly, 'Come on, Principal, we can do this.' I took my position on the centre line of the arena facing the judges, removed my hat and simultaneously bowed my head as is required. I tried to imagine I was back in Smeltings arena just practising my routine, relaxed and calm, just enjoying the moment alone with Prince. It was difficult though. I was amazed how quiet the whole arena fell as I moved off the centreline. You could hear a pin drop, and this in turn made me feel under more pressure to complete the routine with no mistakes. I can still feel the immense sense of relief, trotting up toward the centreline, thinking I'd not made a hash of it, I'd done it. No, actually WE'D done it together, and we were now truly a partnership! My efforts earned Prince and me our first ever rosette together. We finished in sixth place and I was ecstatic!

Christmas at Height

After the euphoria of that weekend, I became a regular on the equestrian competitive circuit. My dressage marks were improving with each competition, and we were taking rosette after rosette. Slowly, but surely, we were climbing to the top of the ladder. Once again in my life the competitive streak in me began to show. At the same time, we were in the throws of bidding for some of the forty-two acres of land which had finally been released onto the market. Unbelievably, it was only a stone's throw from Bassett, a quarter of a mile at the most from our house. Trying to secure the land was an absolute nightmare. We knew right from the start that we would be up against stiff competition. To have forty-two acres of prime land on the market in the Mayfield Valley was virtually unheard of, so it would be very sought after by very many people for all different sorts of reasons. Planning rules and restrictions were becoming more lenient, so the opportunities could be enormous. The one big stumbling block was how the land was being sold. The guidance notes said that the land would be sold off in several different lots by way of closed bids. Our hearts sank. Nigel turned to the estate agents for advice. We didn't want forty-two acres; we couldn't afford forty-two acres, and there was no way of guaranteeing the highest bid for any of the individual lots. In the end I came up with a bit of an unorthodox approach. It was a risk, a long shot but hey, let's give it a go, they could only say no. So that's what we did. We approached the vendor direct.

When all the closed bids were opened we were informed by the estate agents that we had been unsuccessful in making highest bids for any of the lots. We were gutted! However, to our amazement, the following day Nigel received a call from the estate agent. It appeared that the vendor had taken quite a shine to us.

He had been quite taken with my sheer passion and love for these unusual creatures, and he liked the idea of alpacas, BUT, and it was a big BUT, although he was keen to sell to us, he wanted us to purchase the whole forty-two acres!

Now we were in a dilemma; how could we possibly afford it? We couldn't!

Unless...unless we re-mortgaged the house.

The one harsh lesson that the cancer had taught us both, was that we all have only one life, it's no dress rehearsal and sometimes, just sometimes, you need to take risks to 'reach for your dream' whatever the price, whatever the cost. So we did!

We now owned forty-two acres of the picturesque Mayfield Valley. Good grief, it was an exciting but frightening reality! I'm not sure whether it was fear or what, but I can remember laughing hysterically, and saying to Nigel, 'We've only got five alpacas. They're going to look ridiculous on forty two acres.' Nigel agreed, and we fell about laughing.

Nigel wasted no time in drawing up plans to request planning permission to build a 100ft x 40ft American style barn. No driveway existed. A stream, which was running through the proposed building, would have to be diverted and, of course, there was the small matter of several hundred tonnes of soil and rock that had to be excavated to enable the barn to be hidden when erected. Usually, planning permission would be granted by one ruling council but, because the farm is situated in the Mayfield Valley, we are governed by Sheffield City Council as well as Derbyshire Peak Park. At the top of the farm drive we have a Sheffield postcode, but on the opposite side of our drive we are classed as Derbyshire. We couldn't change the situation, so we had no choice but to liaise with both and hope for the best. After weeks and weeks of planning discrepancies we were eventually given the nod; permission was finally granted.

Winter 2000 was pretty much upon us by the time we started major excavation work. It was difficult for Nigel, juggling the stresses and strains that come with business and, at the same time, trying to apply his mind to yet another one of our projects. Nigel's mum and dad would say, 'Oh no, not another project: when are you two going to sit back and relax?' We'd promised ourselves that this was going to be the last one! By mid-December we were making good progress. Nigel thought that, during the week between Christmas and New Year, we would be ready to tackle the erection of the steel framework for the barn. Dads, as always, would be on site to help, and a mutual friend of ours, Andy Gregg, had offered his services, which was very generous of him considering it was during his holiday as well.

On Boxing Day we'd arranged to meet on site at 9am, it was a bitterly cold day, and our thermometer was reading minus four degrees centigrade. Unfortunately, Nigel had come down with an awful cold and had flu-like symptoms. Nevertheless, we were all in good spirits and eager to get started. A Manitou machine had been delivered to site, as that would play a major role in enabling us to reach the twenty-five feet height that would be required to fasten the steel framework together. I had been voted Manitou driver. I'd never driven one before, so I needed a crash course on the finer points of driving a Manitou: well, hopefully not literally! Nigel had constructed a steel man-bucket, which would be connected onto the end of the Manitou's telescopic jib, which in turn would carry Nigel in the bucket high up in the air to fasten the framework together. The set-up was quite amusing as it looked like something off a fireman's lift scene. Joking apart though, it was going to be quite a delicate operation. I felt under enormous pressure to manoeuvre the Manitou's controls with smooth and accurate movements. After all, my husband's safety was literally in my hands.

Hard Graft

It looked like a giant Meccano set! For ease of erection, Nigel had numbered and labelled all the separate pieces of steel for the framework. We'd each been allocated our own job so, after a final briefing from Nigel, we all knew the sequence of events, what we had to do and when we had to do it. 'Practical' should be Nigel's middle name, because one of my Christmas presents was a set of walkie talkies. We needed some way of communicating with each other over the sound of machinery and contractors plant, so Nigel decided that walkie talkies would be ideal. Don't get me wrong; I'm not at all adverse to practical presents, but it just epitomises the essence of how an engineer's mind works. One year, when we were very much into our sailing, Nigel bought me a Bosun's chair for Christmas. This traditionally consists of a plank of wood encapsulated with canvas, with two pieces of rope attached to an eyelet. A crew member can then hoist his fellow crew member up the mast to sort out any high level problems (i.e. electrical, or rope work). It came as no surprise to me when Nigel reasoned that there was no way I was strong enough to haul his fifteen stone frame up the mast! No prizes for guessing who was going up the mast then!

I wouldn't say the Manitou was a difficult machine to drive, but the joystick which moved the telescopic beam was highly sensitive. One incorrect move on the joystick, and Nigel could have been fireman Sam no longer.

'You'll be fine,' Nigel reassured me. 'Just take your time, and think what you're doing before you do it. You've driven a dumper truck before.'

'Oh, great, no probs then, should be a doddle,' I replied sarcastically, as I climbed into the cab. Once the frames had been assembled on the ground we were ready to lift them into place.

Nigel hooked the webbing strap onto the Manitou and gave me instructions over the walkie talkie to start lifting. I was as nervous as hell, but I knew it was down to me. I couldn't expect dads to take on the responsibility, and Nigel and Andy had their own part to play. All credit to Nigel, the frames slotted onto the bolts on the ground with such accuracy. Once the first frame was in place, we all had a much better idea of what we were doing. The one problem that still remained was that we still had to remove the strap from the hook on the teleporter. This seemed a good time to have a tea break whilst we deliberated how we could achieve this. With cup of tea in hand, we all looked skyward toward the hook and strop that were swaying in the wind. Nigel broke the silence when he said, 'Well, the only way to remove it is by ladder. I can't think of any other option. The frame won't take that much weight on it, though, because it's only held up by the bolts on the ground.' I didn't know whether to laugh or cry when everyone's gaze turned towards me. After all, it was obvious, I weighed less by far; silly me for not offering sooner!

Several months into construction and it was beginning to look something like a farm, although the work was taking its toll on all of us. The one job we did contract out was the roof and the concrete flooring. Jim, a bricklayer and a friend of Nigel's, had previously done some work for us on Bassett, so was called in to erect the two-metre wall around the barn. The timber boarding that sat on top of the external wall turned out to be such a laborious job. Nigel and I nailed hundreds and hundreds of six-inch wide Yorkshire boards on. They butted up to the base of the roof, with several nails in each board. That's a lot of nails! One of the last jobs to do was to install alpaca pens and stabling. Costs were beginning to escalate at quite an alarming rate by now. We had limited resources available, hence the reason why we completed most of the work ourselves. Summertime 2001 and we had turned our attentions to the outdoor work. Further excavations, outdoor arenas, field separation, stock fencing and, of course, the alpacas. I'd promised myself that I must find time to take my two girls back down to Bozedown to get them covered. Part of the original purchase price included 50% off stud fees for first time returning customers. I was keen to start increasing my herd numbers, so I was determined to put the girls in calf. Considering that the gestation period is fifty weeks, I had to sort it sooner rather than later. I'd kept in touch with Joy at Bozedown, and we spoke fairly regularly over the phone. There were many times when I needed advice and, to be fair to Joy, she was always willing to lend an ear and help in any way she could.

Joy had shown a great deal of interest in the purchase of the land. 'Forty-two acres is a substantial smallholding to own,' I remember her saying to me feeling rather panicked. I'm sure Joy presumed we'd got a plan in mind to put the land to use, but actually we hadn't at all. I suppose we'd bought it on a bit of a whim, although I was too embarrassed to admit that. In the end, I never had to make the trip down to Oxfordshire, as Joy and Ken (Joy's husband) were due to make a trip up country to visit their associate breeders. Joy very kindly offered to bring the two studs I'd chosen for my girls along with them in the trailer, in return for a bed for the night. It benefited both of us, so that's what we agreed. Joy Whitehead was a big name in the UK Alpaca industry, and I suppose I was inspired by what she had already achieved. If I could be half as successful as Joy had been then that would be fine by me. Joy and Ken were lovely people, very well spoken and from visiting their home on several occasions, it was obvious that they had done very nicely for themselves. Ken was a retired British Airways pilot and, although he had retired a few years earlier, he still loved his flying. He owned a modern light aircraft and a historic bi-plane, you know, just like most folk!

The biplane was housed in a small aircraft hanger, which was part of their one hundred and twenty acre site, along with their home. On one occasion Nigel and myself were sat in their kitchen eating Joy's homemade soup, when Ken suddenly jumped up from the table, looking at his watch saying, 'Crikey, is that the time? I really must fly.' We thought nothing of it at the time; it was just a figure of speech. Fifteen minutes later we heard the sound of really loud engines nearby and Joy said, 'Oh, don't look so worried, it'll be Ken. I'll just see him off.' 'See him off?' I whispered to Nigel, 'He went ages ago'. We must have looked absolutely star-struck as we gaped out of the window. Joy was on the lawn waving madly as Ken was just taxiing past ready for take off in his historic bi-plane. We stood there in amazement, watching this unbelievable scene unfold in front of our eyes. There was Ken on the controls, with his Biggles helmet and goggles on, and scarf flailing behind him. Honestly, it looked like a sketch from the cartoon series, 'Wacky Races'. When Ken had said, 'I really must fly,' we never imagined he meant literally! We couldn't stop laughing all the way home.

Pastures New

It seemed as though we'd been talking about the farm for ever.

There had been so many aspects of the build that we had tackled, so many construction problems that we'd had to overcome, and still so much more to do.

We had eaten, drunk and slept the farm for such a long time that it all came as a bit of a shock when one day we realised we were very nearly there!

Joy Whitehead had stopped off at Sheffield to stay overnight at Bassett on a couple of occasions whilst travelling around the country to see her associate breeders. These were like-minded alpaca people who had become associated with Bozedown Alpacas, in order to benefit from the excellent reputation that Joy had developed, and also to gain access to the superb pool of genetics that was present in the Bozedown herd. The reciprocal benefit from Bozedown's point of view was that they received a twenty five percent cut from the profit generated from each transaction.

Considering that we were at such an early stage of our development, our facilities had obviously made a big impression on Joy for her to invite us to become one of her northern associate breeders. The facilities were now physically in place. What I lacked were some alpacas to sell, as well as hands-on experience with the finer points of alpaca breeding. Joy provided the solution to this problem by offering to loan us our initial sales stock after I completed a weeks tutoring by Joy at Bozedown Alpaca farm. Obviously, I jumped at the opportunity to spend some quality time learning my trade from someone who I considered to be tutor and mentor. Both my girls were heavily pregnant by now, and I was keen to have some hands-on experience birthing crias, before I had it all to do on my own farm in the coming weeks.

Two weeks later, mid-July 2002, I tentatively climbed into Nigel's silver Mitsubishi Shogun to make the four-and-a-half hour drive down to Bozedown in Oxfordshire.

Unfortunately I had been in the wars again. My neck was in a rigid neck collar!

Ever since the prolapsed disc in my lower back had been operated on, another disc in my neck had been detected on the MRI Scan as being slightly prolapsed. Every now and then it would flare up and, apart from anti-inflammatory and pain killers, there wasn't much I could do about it apart from waiting for it to ease.

Both mums were horrified to hear that I was still insistent on making the trip to Oxfordshire, but even Nigel couldn't deter me. This trip alone for me would be a first, as I'd never spent a night away from Nigel since we'd been married, apart from my unavoidable stays in hospital. I'd never even driven on a motorway on my own, so this was scary stuff, and I must admit to being quite anxious about the whole thing. Nevertheless, I was determined to keep to our arrangement. In the end the drive down was fairly non-eventful. Nigel had written down all the directions to reach Bozedown, and I made several stops for refreshments, as he'd suggested. In fact I really quite enjoyed singing along to the Tom Jones CD that I'd bought from the services. Nigel had rung me on several occasions during the journey to make sure I was okay and still on track with his directions. I know it seems ridiculous, but this was a big event for me, and I was pretty proud of myself when I finally turned into the village of Whitchurch. I'd reached my destination without any hitches. All I had to do now was check in at the White Hart public house, and relax for the rest of the evening. This was to be my home for the next seven days.

The following morning the alarm clock woke me at 6.30am prompt. I washed, dressed and made my way down to the small restaurant that I'd eaten in the night before. This morning it had been transformed into a breakfast room. However, I was excited about the forthcoming day's events, so much so that the butterflies in my tummy suppressed my appetite. Nevertheless, I did my best to demolish as much of the cooked breakfast as I could possibly manage. I didn't know when I would next eat, so thought it best to stock up on energy, and the old saying of 'breakfast like a King' sprung to mind. The short journey to Bozedown took no longer than two or three minutes by car. I had contemplated walking there, but decided against it, considering I might be grateful to just flop into the car on my return journey later, depending on how hard I'd been worked during the day.

Apart from that, the weather was boiling hot and the walk to the farm was all uphill. As I approached the farm, the familiar site of alpacas grazing was welcoming. The peaceful nature of alpacas always made me feel calm, and I felt a warm glow inside. What incredible creatures they were, and how fortunate I had been to have them enhance my life when I so needed them. Perhaps the man upstairs was looking out for me after all. Mary-Jo, Joy's niece and second-in-command, was there to greet me. Mary-Jo is Canadian, a confident, short, buxom lady with a big personality. She'd been working alongside Joy for a few years now and, although primarily office-based, she was extremely knowledgeable about alpacas. I'd met Mary-Jo on a number of occasions and, although I liked her, I must admit to being slightly overawed by her extrovert personality and confident manner. This may have been partly down to me, as back then I was a very different person from the person I am today. Seventeen years ago I was shy, nervous, inexperienced but, most of all, I didn't have an ounce of self-esteem. Mary-Jo appeared to me to be everything I wasn't and I was envious of that. However, she knew her stuff, and I respected her for that.

The majority of the morning was spent familiarising myself with the layout of the farm in general: how the paddocks had been separated, catch pen areas, segregation of males/females, nursing paddocks and so on. I was shown where feeds were made up, various veterinary vaccines that were used on site, and what they were used for, whilst all the time making notes to further my understanding of what would be required of me if I was to be responsible and successful in running a similar operation. By the end of the first day I was knackered, not so much physically, but mentally. I was pleased that I'd made the decision to drive myself to the farm and not walk there, although it would have been all downhill on the return journey!

That evening I rang Nigel to tell him about the day's events. I was tired, but I was also on a high. I was full of it. For once in my life I was doing something for me, something that I was passionate about, something that I never thought I would find, contentment.

Mayfield Alpacas – Open for Business

The following days were invaluable in my early business education. I listened and learned from Joy, she was a good teacher, and her love of alpacas shone through.

She was a talented businesswoman in her own right, but her genuine love of alpacas was obvious. Mary-Jo, on the other hand, seemed much more matter of fact.

I can remember, on one occasion during that week, a cria had been born to a young female, but sadly it was born with a deformity. It had what we call a 'wry' face, which is basically a disfiguration of the face which means that the teeth do not align properly. This means that the alpaca would probably never be able to eat sufficient amounts of food, and then would not be able to 'chew the cud' to digest anything properly. So it could face much future suffering. Mary-Jo was of the opinion that it should be culled (humanely killed) immediately. Joy was not happy when she suggested it. Neither was I. It's never an easy decision. However, on this occasion, nature made the decision for Bozedown as, sadly, the little cria died later on that same day. But if we thought that this little cria could never live out a normal, healthy life due to its deformity then, as responsible breeders, we would have had to face up to making a hard decision. My love and passion for these animals means more to me than solely running a successful business. I suppose in the true sense of the word you could say I'm not your typical 'businesswoman'. Maybe some would argue I am not, but what I am is satisfied in the knowledge that I am true to myself and the animals that I care for.

Towards the end of the week, I was feeling more and more confident about dealing with the different situations that I could be faced with at some time in the future. I felt like a sponge; the more I absorbed the more I wanted to learn. I began questioning

Joy about all the different aspects of alpaca psychology and physiology; you name it, I asked it. I couldn't have blamed Joy if, by the end of the week, she had been pleased to see the back of me. I'd certainly been testing her knowledge and, at times, I think she was aware of that.

I suppose, for me, the highlight of the week had to be hands-on birthing a cria. Even now, after all these years, assisting a dam (female alpaca) to help deliver her cria is one of the most emotional and rewarding tasks I have ever done. Nature is a fascinating phenomenon and one which never ceases to amaze me. To watch a dam encourage her newborn cria to stand reduces me to tears every time. She'll caress and gently hum to her newborn, giving little nudges of encouragement, whilst all the time guarding her precious baby with her life. Alpacas are very social creatures, and all female alpacas like to play a part in welcoming the latest newcomer to their herd. They all gather round at a birth to greet the new arrival with great interest, sometimes at the disapproval of mum. If aunties get too close, mum will retaliate with a spit as if to say, 'Back off, too close for comfort.' If an inquisitive cria does the same he/she will be rebuffed with a spit and a nibble as if to say, 'Clear off, my property.'

On the whole though, most females will happily live together in harmony and look out for each other; after all, having a baby is quite a big deal.

It was late July 2002, Nigel had rung me at 8.00am to let me know that he was on his way down to Bozedown to collect me and our little herd of twelve alpacas. I'd missed Nigel loads over the past week and I was so looking forward to seeing him. I'd so much I wanted to tell him and talk to him about, I was almost bursting. Finally, around 12.30pm, my blue Mitsubishi Shogun appeared out of the tree-lined lane with a six-wheeler livestock trailer on tow. Again, our good neighbours had come to our rescue and had generously offered to lend us their brand new trailer for our own use. It was difficult trying to restrain myself from rushing up to Nigel and throwing my arms around him, but I thought better of it since there was quite a large audience of staff around. Instead we warmly hugged each other as I whispered,

'Love you.' Nigel reciprocated by kissing my head and answering 'Me you too.'

We didn't want to waste too much time loading the alpacas, as we still had a long drive back to Sheffield, and with twelve animals in the trailer it was going to be quite a tight squeeze. Joy was there to oversee the loading and, to be fair to the alpacas, they walked into the trailer like the animals in Noah's Ark, two by two.

The paperwork and agreement had been dealt with before we loaded the animals, so all that remained was to say our thanks and goodbyes, and we were on our way.

Looking back to that day now, I have so much to be grateful to Joy for. In essence, Joy provided me with the opportunity to stand on my own two feet from day one.

She was putting her trust in me to take away twelve of her own alpacas, to be cared for by me. I was naïve, green and, above all else, very new to such an enterprise; only time would tell if I would survive.

I think if I had known back then what I know now, I would have been less likely to achieve what I have done with Mayfield Alpacas. Mayfield Alpacas has evolved, literally, day by day, week by week, month by month, and year on year. It might sound ridiculous, but I don't think I ever really sat back and took the time to think what I was getting myself into. Maybe if I had done I would have run a mile. That balmy July evening, when we unlocked the back of the trailer to unload the Bozedown animals, became a turning point in my life from alpaca hobbyist to the successful businesswoman that I am today.

Nigel's Dad – A True Gentleman

I was rapidly approaching another milestone in my life: my fortieth Birthday.

Some months earlier the usual team, which consisted of Nigel's dad, my dad, Nigel and I, were struggling to unload the steel purling that would form part of the steel framework for the barn roof. As I recall, it was a windy November day and, from the back of my Shogun, several tonnes of steel swung precariously at the end of a heavy duty strap. Although this was proving to be quite a tricky manoeuvre, all seemed well until a gust of wind swung the load towards the back of my car. Dad instinctively put his hand up to steady the swinging steel, and his left hand was punched through the back window of my car. Although the injury did not seem too severe we took advice from a consultant surgeon, who recommended an exploratory operation to make sure that the tendons in dad's wrist were not damaged. Pre-operative routine blood tests revealed that, unbeknown to us all, dad was suffering from a blood condition known as Mylodisplasia, commonly referred to as pre–Leukaemia. This diagnosis dropped a bombshell for all of us, and explained dad's declining health over the previous months. I can neither convey, nor try in a few sentences, to express the aching sadness which we all felt.

Nigel's dad was a very brave and proud man, but the debilitating disease took its toll over the following months, culminating ultimately in dad's death in October 2003, just two weeks after my fortieth birthday. In dad's early career as a headmaster, he was highly acclaimed for pioneering new ways of teaching children with limited language skills. Dad was no snob, and never discriminated against less fortunate people. In the old-fashioned sense of the word he described himself as a true socialist, believing throughout his life that, as a community, we should all work towards the improvement of the lives of those less fortunate than ourselves. My dad described Nigel's dad as, 'A true gentleman'. Never was this more aptly spoken.

In the aftermath of dad's death I busied myself trying to support Nigel's mum and indeed Nigel himself. I'd lost someone who I held very dear to my heart, but Mum had lost her husband of over forty years, and Nigel had lost his dad. It was a horrendous time in all our lives but, for me, I was hindered by the dreaded cloud of depression and OCD that had begun to approach me once again. I tried so hard to push it away, I really did. I'd talk out loud to myself, 'Don't fold now, Elaine; don't give in, and don't let it win.' But it did win. It engulfed me like a tornado.

Several dismal weeks followed. I hated myself for my weakness. Nigel and his mum became my carers like so many times before. Nigel decided he had no option other than to hire in the help of Vicky and Smeltings Farm. Prince (my horse) and the alpacas needed to be looked after, as well as my ducks and geese. Nigel was full-on running his own business (Airflow) and then, taking over from mum in the evening, looking after me. He certainly hadn't the time or energy to be mucking out horses and alpacas. Vicky, as always, was prepared to lend a helping hand wherever possible, and she did. Eventually my condition improved, and with that some form of normality resumed over a period of time. I wasn't yet well enough to cope with major decisions, but I was getting there, albeit slowly.

Bring it on

I got my first lucky break only a few weeks after moving up to the farm. We had transferred our original five alpacas to the farm, as there didn't seem any point in not doing. After all, there were still only seventeen alpacas on forty-two acres: oh, and Prince, my horse. The internal infrastructure of the barn was still some way off being completed, but we always knew that it was not going to happen overnight. The project would take a great deal of money to fund, so we had to cut according to our cloth; and so early on in the business' infancy, we didn't have much cloth to cut with! As luck would have it, I'd been introduced, some six months earlier, to a lady who was interested in alpacas. So, I took the bull by the horns and put a call through to the lady in question, Lorna Hunter. I felt I had nothing to lose, but everything to gain, she could always say no. Remarkably, she said yes. After making arrangements with Lorna, I eagerly looked forward to meeting her the following weekend at the farm. 'Remember,' Nigel had said when I excitedly told him, 'it's not a sale until you have the money. Make sure you get a deposit from her to secure the animals.' 'I know, I know, but I'm halfway there, aren't I, if she's coming to look?' I replied. 'Oh, love,' Nigel said, 'you've got a lot to learn, don't be too disappointed if she doesn't go for it.'

Nigel's concerns, fortunately for me, were unfounded. Lorna signed up for six pregnant females. The only problem was that the females were not pregnant. I reassured Lorna that I would put the girls into calf as soon as possible with suitable stud males, all of which would be unrelated. Obviously, from a breeding perspective, it was important that the females were impregnated with different studs, so future pregnancies would create a wider gene pool for Lorna. Also, I would have to arrange with Joy to collect another white pregnant female from Bozedown, as I had not got sufficient white animals to sell myself at this stage. Lorna was happy and I was ecstatic! The sale totalled around £28.000 plus VAT. Wow, what a start!

Nigel's initial reaction to my first sale was, well, let's just say he was gob-smacked; actually so was I. If only I could have known that not all business deals run so smoothly.

The alpacas had begun to cause quite an interest at the farm. In the early days we had to rebuild our dry-stone wall about a dozen times. So many drivers took their eyes off the road to look at the strange, woolly, long-legged animals that graced our paddocks, and inadvertently ran straight into the wall at the top of the farm drive. We found this rather amusing but the drivers did not!

It was, similarly, one of these occasions when the alpacas were spotted, quite by chance, by a freelance journalist. Penny Baddeley was a pretty, slim, ginger-haired lady with lots of freckles. Her daily commute involved passing our farm and, when the alpacas were established in our paddocks, she thought what a great story this would make for our local newspaper, the then 'Sheffield Star and Telegraph'.

The completed article was front page news, entitled 'Unusual Animals in Ringinglow'.

(Co-incidentally, years later I taught Penny's son, James, who came to me from university as part of his training to become a vet).

This would be the first of many newspaper articles, radio interviews and television interviews to come over the following months and years. I'd had a tiny taste of the limelight some years earlier when I was training for the 'Star Walk', which of course I did win. Being the daughter of an ex-Olympian I did stir up quite a deal of interest. However, I couldn't have anticipated in my wildest dreams the interest which my latest venture would cause.

Before I get ahead of myself, there was still the small matter of my first sale to complete, so we'll back-track to that first.

Okay, yes, the sale. I telephoned Joy to tell her the good news. 'Well done, Elaine,' said a surprised voice. 'That's a large sum of money by any standards'. I imagined Joy on the other end of the phone calculating the inevitable 75% of the sale that would, in due course be coming her way. After all, if it wasn't for

Joy's generosity I wouldn't be in the fortunate position of being associated with Bozedown and, believe you me, being under the Bozedown umbrella was a pretty big deal for me.

Joy was a lovely lady, but also a very shrewd businesswoman. I made arrangements to collect another white pregnant female the following week, from another associate breeder in the north of England, as that would save me time and money on a nine-hour round trip, plus fuel. Again, and fortunately for me, a member of Joy's staff had to drive the tortuous route all the way up to Aberdeen to make a delivery of alpacas, so it was suggested that they could pick up the last alpaca for Lorna and deliver it straight to her on the return trip, which was more or less en route from Aberdeen. I was completely happy with that. In essence, it didn't quite turn out as straightforward as I had hoped. It was early September and, as usual, the majority of alpacas in the UK had been shorn by then, mine included (alpacas are sheared once a year). However, alpacas can, and do, look quite weird once they have had their fleece removed. Have you seen the spectacles advert with the farmer and Border Collie dog? I apologise to those who have, but for those who haven't it goes like this: a hill farmer shears his sheep but, because he needs a new pair of specs, he also shears his border collie by mistake. The look of embarrassment and indignation on the dog's face is superlative! Well, that's just like the alpacas. They look nude and a shadow of their former self, apart from a large tuft of fleece on the top of their head. (This is for weather protection and is called the top-knot).

Anyway, back to the story, the first thing I heard was when Lorna rang me in a bit of a state. Apparently, yes, they had delivered the alpaca but, to Lorna's amazement, it had got what she described as large yellow spots on it!!! I was bemused, but surely I was hearing things; was this another breed of the lesser-spotted alpaca that I hadn't come across until now?

The outcome, it turned out, was quite an innocent one and, once I had made the short trip over to Lorna's farm in Harrogate, all was revealed. The alpaca in question had been treated for some areas of hair loss after shearing, hence the bright yellow cream dotted on strategic parts of the alpaca's body. I could understand Lorna's immediate concerns though, it did look rather odd!

Anyway, all's well that ends well and, after the initial shock and explanation, we were able to have a good laugh about the whole situation.

Business of the Year Award

The sales just kept on coming. As the sales kept on coming, so did the publicity, so did my reputation as a highly regarded alpaca breeder, which culminated in my business acumen being noticed. Over the years I had always been frustrated that I had never realised my true potential. I knew that I had it in me, but I didn't know what was needed to get it out. I know now, it was passion. I suppose my first taste of self-satisfaction came a few years earlier. Everything Nigel and I have embarked upon has been completed to as high a standard as possible. Our sailing exams were one such example. It seemed bizarre to me that the law allows a person to buy a boat and head out to sea without the necessity to have any formal training or qualifications. We were determined that this was not going to be the way for us. However, neither did I anticipate that Nigel would set us up for three years at night school, as well as several classroom exams; oh, and, of course, all the practical exams to boot. Yes, he certainly intended to be thorough! Joking apart though, as I have said before, the sea takes no prisoners, it needs treating with far more respect than sometimes people give it. Fortunately for me I did have the additional home tuition from Nigel. I think I would have struggled far more with the technical aspects of the chart work and navigational theory if Nigel had not been there to guide me. Nevertheless, I was immensely proud of myself to pass the exam alone, and to ultimately become a qualified skipper. On the evening that I received my results, I cried. I cried tears of happiness, but I also cried tears from years of self doubt. Nigel cried with me, and so did his dad. They knew what it meant to me, not just all the hard work for a pass, they knew what the pass meant for my self esteem.

It was whilst we were in Jersey that I received the call. We had sold Juliet, our twenty-four foot sailing boat, for a larger version. The equity we had in Juliet enabled us to purchase a hull and deck moulding for another sailing boat, a 'Countess 35', which we named 'Ocean Breeze'. Never shy of a challenge, we yet again set about completing another project. The project would see us out of the water for two years in total. It was a frustrating time. We wanted to be out sailing, but we also wanted a larger boat. We couldn't afford to buy the finished article without taking on a marine mortgage, and we certainly didn't want the pressure of another mortgage, so when all else fails 'we build it', simple as that, or not!

At the time of delivery we were still living on Dobcroft Road. She (a boat is always classed as a lady) was shoe-horned into our front garden with inches to spare. At just over 35ft she took command of our small front garden! The night she arrived was a bitterly cold December evening with a heavy frost. I'm still grateful to this day that it was night-time, as our neighbours would have thought an unidentified flying object was landing. It was certainly a tight squeeze. The following morning, when our neighbours opened their curtains, they must have done a double take. 'Is it a bird? Is it a plane? No, it's our nutty neighbours again!' Let's put it this way, Ocean Breeze definitely gave people something to talk about; she became a local landmark in the area!

Anyway, back to the phone call. Joy and David were on board holidaying with us (Joy, my riding companion, not Joy at Bozedown)). We were planning to sail over to St Malo in France for a few days. The forecast was good and the weather was settled. We had made the trip a few times before, but not with Joy and David. Joy had expressed her concerns over the seven-hour passage, so I was determined to make the trip as hassle-free and as enjoyable as possible for her. Chart-work was something I had to do, as I needed to practise a fair bit to make sure I remembered what I been taught. It just came so easily to Nigel, which did annoy me a tad; I suppose I was jealous really. Nevertheless, I had to keep my hand in, and whilst I was doing just that at the chart table I answered my mobile, 'Good morning, Mayfield Alpacas.'

The voice on the other end was a man's. It turned out that he was ringing from the Sheffield Chamber of Commerce.

We had previously worked with Business Link South Yorkshire in connection with some grant funding for the alpaca visitor centre at the farm. Unbeknown to us, Business Link had been contacted by the Chamber and asked if they knew of any rapidly expanding local businesses that had a good business plan and an interesting product. I listened to what the man had to say. 'We would like to put Mayfield Alpacas forward for the Yorkshire business awards'. You can imagine my surprise, it couldn't be anything to do with me, I thought: and not my little business. He must have dialled an incorrect number, but hang on, he mentioned Mayfield Alpacas by name. Indeed, after asking him again, the penny finally dropped; actually it did seem to be me he wanted. So, after picking myself up from the saloon floor, I listened to what he'd got to say with some amazement. Apparently, he told me, I'd been recommended by Business Link, and could I submit a business plan, trading accounts and other supporting documentation. With Nigel's help we sent off the information and thought that would be that.

A month or so later I received another phone call to say we had been short-listed, and that we were invited to attend the presentation awards at a local venue called Baldwin's. We knew Baldwin's very well. It was the venue where we had held our wedding reception all those years ago; only back then it was called the Omega, still owned by local business man David Baldwin. It was a posh place and we were told that the dress code was 'black tie'. My first thought was, 'What a waste of time, surely a micro business like ours had no hope of competing with the giants of industry and the modern high technology businesses working in computing and medicine?'

Nigel and I debated whether we should bother going but, to our surprise, a week before the awards we were told we had been short-listed for an award of some kind. The awards night came. It was a 'formal do'. All the men were in their best bib and tucker and the ladies in all their finery, 'posh frocks'. We didn't really know what to expect, but immediately, as we got out of the taxi, we sensed that this would be no ordinary evening for us. Wayne Paige worked for Business Link, and was the chap who had assisted us in securing the grant funding for the visitor centre some months earlier. Wayne was there to meet us at the main entrance, and then ushered us through to the suite where the Dinner and presentations were to take place later on in the evening. Nigel's mum accompanied us, along with Joy and David, as we had been given some complimentary tickets by Business Link. The champagne was flowing, and we were all handed a glass before Nigel and myself were swept off to be introduced to the 'big wigs' from the chamber. I shook hands with so many people that my arm was beginning to ache. Every now and again a photographer would ask us to pose for a photograph with the various different people we were being introduced to. At the time I did think it seemed quite strange that we were attracting a fair bit of attention, but to be honest I was quite enjoying it. Dinner was finally announced by the bang of a gong, and everyone was asked to take their seats.

The function room was laid out with round tables that seated about ten people. Our little group consisted of the five of us, Wayne and his wife, and three others who we had only been introduced to earlier. Whenever Baldwin's host a formal dinner, you know you're in for a real treat. David Baldwin, the owner and head chef, is always very hands-on to maintain his impeccable standards of food and silver service. Tonight would be no exception. After saying grace, everyone tucked in to the beautifully presented cold seafood platter - it was delicious. Next was the soup course, cream of chicken and mushroom with hot crusty roll and butter. Dinner was to be five courses but, because I was both a little nervous and excited, I had already started to panic about not finishing my meal. I had always been brought up to clear my plate; being wasteful cost money and it had been hard-earned by my dad. Nevertheless, portion sizes were not over-zealous with so many courses, so I didn't do too badly.

Main course was traditional roast beef with Yorkshire pudding, finished off with a choice of either chocolate soufflé or fresh fruit salad. Cheese and biscuits followed, accompanied with port or a liquor of your choice, and finally coffee and mints. By the end of dinner everyone seemed relaxed and happy, people were chatting and laughing and obviously enjoying the evening. Mind you, the alcohol does wonders for a bit of Dutch courage.

The first person to interrupt the laughter was a gentleman, whom I presumed was part of the Chamber. A microphone had been placed immediately at the side of their table. After a quick tap of the microphone to test for sound he said, 'Ladies and Gentleman.' He must have realised he needed to speak louder, as he repeated, 'Ladies and Gentleman, please may I have your attention. It gives me great pleasure,' and he was off into his well-prepared spiel. The next lady to be introduced to us all was a tall redheaded lady called, Julia Gash. In the 1990's Julia Gash was one of Sheffield's leading businesswomen, designing fashion for the young and selling it to the Far East. She won export awards, showed Princess Anne around her factory and had tea at Buckingham Palace. In 2000 she launched Gash, a website and shop specialising in erotica!

'Crikey,' I thought, 'tea at the palace, no pressure there then.'

It seemed to me that Ms Gash and I were very different people. I would no sooner be spotted wandering around an erotica shop than, I dare say, neither would Julia Gash probably be spotted up to her knees in muck working on a farm. Heigh-ho, it wouldn't do for us all to be the same. However, we did have one very fundamental vision in common, and I think that was the word 'passion' again. Passion for our vocation, and passion for what we were trying to achieve. She too had been dealt a difficult hand in business some years previous, but she survived.

She survived, I believe, because of passion and that single-minded determination to carry on fighting, never giving in even when the odds are stacked against you. I do truly believe you have to have hope, whether it is facing a personal financial crisis or a personal medical condition. In similar ways they both knock your world sideways, but you still need hope, and sometimes, just sometimes, something comes along to make sense of all the madness! This is my opinion anyway, because I lived through it. That evening in Baldwin's was surreal.

'And, the winner of the 2004 Business award of the year goes to Elaine Sharp of Mayfield Alpacas'. The sound of my name and Mayfield Alpacas resonated in my head. I was dumfounded, stunned, but above all, for a few seconds I doubted what I thought I'd just heard. Was I dreaming? Reality took over only when Nigel took my arm to encourage me to get out of my chair. Everyone was looking at me, and they were clapping, smiling and nodding simultaneously. It was unbelievable. Nigel, with his arm around my shoulder, leaned towards me and kissed my head and whispered, 'Well done, girl.' With a gentle hand on my back he reassuringly urged me to go forward to receive my prize. As I glanced back to look at him, I will never forget the look of love and pride in his eyes, as he remained standing clapping with everyone else. In my head I was saying, 'I couldn't have done it without you, Bun.'

What Next?

There's a well-known saying, often used in the business world, which is 'success breeds success'. In hindsight that's just what happened to Mayfield Alpacas in the Chamber of Commerce Business awards. Shortly after the euphoria of my win in the Yorkshire awards, I was informed by 'Business Link' that they wanted to submit our business through to represent Yorkshire in the National awards. Apart from feeling very flattered, I felt I had nothing to lose as all the hard preparation work had already been done. The presentation ceremony was to be held in London but, as we were absolutely certain we wouldn't stand a chance, we didn't even bother travelling down to attend! Big mistake. When the news came to say we had actually won we were all totally dumbfounded!

Winning the UK final meant that we went forward to the World finals which were to be held this year in Tokyo. Needless to say we were not placed in the top three, but for Mayfield Alpacas to be put forward to represent our country was, for me, accolade enough.

Considering I was primarily an alpaca breeder, and breeding top quality alpacas was the mainstay of my business, I began gathering different species around me. From the early part of my diagnosis I started off with ducks, and then the goslings arrived. Ducks are beautiful, comical things, and the more time I spent around them the more I came to love them. They waddled around our garden, splashed in the pond and genuinely made us all smile. Mums adored them, so much so that every Saturday they would wander out into the garden to feed them brown bread, which they'd bought for them. All my ducks became familiar with us, they were all given names and often they would happily eat out of our hands. I became a member of the Poultry

Society of Great Britain, and regularly Nigel and I would go off to shows at weekends. One year Nigel bought me an incubator for my birthday. I fancied collecting the eggs from my ducks and incubating them myself, so Nigel took it upon himself to source the correct incubator for small-scale breeders. I was thrilled, and thirty-five days later I had a variety of breeds of call ducks. I was even there to video their birth. I kept a close eye on the eggs once they were near to hatching and, sure enough, at around 2.00am one Friday morning, I saw several of the eggs starting to crack near to where the ducklings were 'pippin' through the shell with their egg tooth. I cried, it was amazing to watch. I'd never experienced anything being born into this world before; well, only on television, and there's no comparison to watching it in real life.

Once the business was becoming established, I decided that it made sense to move my ducks up to the farm. I missed not having them around. I'd become accustomed to them, and wanted them to enjoy their massive playground of forty-two acres. Prince, too, was introduced to his new home. The barn housed several custom-made stables, built by ourselves, and Prince settled in like an old hand. He had always been the laid-back type and reasonably happy to be on his own, which most horses are not. However, I did advertise that livery was available, and it wasn't long before another two or three horses joined us on the farm. Prince was as happy as a sandboy with his new friends, but always remained top of the pecking order, and still has done to this day, despite his twenty-two years.

Whilst my little empire was gradually expanding, I was mindful of the fact that, if I was ever to hit the big-time breeding alpacas, I was going to need a substantial influx of alpacas on the farm. Gestation period being fifty weeks made rapid expansion a non-starter. I would have to approach this with some intelligence, and I thought I might just have a plan. Joy Whitehead, from Bozedown Alpacas, had already imported some alpacas and was about to do the same again. If I could tap in to Joy's knowledge and skill of doing so, why couldn't I? It transpired that this group of alpacas would be of supreme quality, and supposedly the best group of alpacas ever imported into the UK. If anyone could organise it, then that anyone was Joy, and I wanted to be a part of it. With all Joy's contacts and previous experience, this was an opportunity not to be missed. The plan was to fly out to Peru where we would be met by guides, who would then to take us high into the mountains to seek out the premium alpaca farms at high altitude. No hotels would exist where we were bound for, sleeping under canvas would become our home for fourteen nights, and a once in a lifetime experience of being truly at one with nature.

However, it was not to be. Three weeks before the trip my health once again let me down as it had done so many times in the past. My immune system was already compromised because of the full removal of my lymph nodes during my breast surgery. It would appear that I probably contracted some kind of infection whilst working at the farm and, consequently, with no lymph glands to drain out the fluid, the infection just stagnated in my arm. The symptoms at first were fairly insignificant, apart from a mild discomfort in my left wrist and lower arm; until a feeling of sheer exhaustion started to sweep over me. I left work at lunchtime, showered and climbed into bed. Three hours later I awoke to an agonising pain in the whole of my left arm, together with a burning sensation. I can only liken it to hot steam escaping from a boiling kettle; it was so painful even to touch lightly. 'Jesus Christ,' I whimpered, 'what the hell's wrong with me?' My thoughts were interrupted by the sound of a car's engine. Raising my head off the pillow I glanced to my right to see the bright green numbers emitting from our digital clock/radio; the time was showing 5.36pm. 'Thank goodness,' I thought, 'he's early for once.' 'Hi, love,' Nigel shouted, as he came through the porch door into the dining room. 'Bun, I'm down here in bed, can you come?' I replied.

The brightness of the main light being switched on by Nigel made me squint for a few seconds. I sat up in bed, cradling my left arm in my right, and Nigel sat down next to me and stared at my arm. 'What the - what's happened?' he said, as he continued staring at my arm. 'Not very well, bun,' I groaned. After a brief explanation Nigel picked up the phone and rang Mr Shorthouse (my breast cancer surgeon). Five minutes later I was being bundled into the car en-route to Riverdale Road, Mr Shorthouse's home address. It took only a matter of seconds for Mr Shorthouse to diagnose the problem. I had contracted septicaemia! (Also more commonly known as blood poisoning.)

Events rather overtook me after that. Nigel drove me the short distance to Thornbury Hospital to be admitted onto a ward. Guess which one… Yes, it was Mappin again. By the time we arrived Mr Shorthouse was already there. He'd made all the necessary arrangements and I was ushered immediately to the ward, where several medical staff were on hand to assist. I was deteriorating rapidly by this stage. I was feeling faint and sick and desperately wanted to lie down. My shoulder and chest were now hurting, and my legs felt like I'd just run a back-to-back marathon. I can remember some sort of large machinery being wheeled into the room; it was grey in colour and had a glass side. That's all I can remember before darkness took me over, and I passed out.

And There's More

The newly completed 'Coffee Shop' June 2006

When I finally came to, I was hooked up to a drip with an individual monitor on the side of it. Bleeps and buzzers were emanating from various pieces of machinery, and an oxygen mask was strapped over my nose and mouth. I felt as though I was being suffocated, so I was reaching up to remove the mask, when I heard a voice say, 'Hey you, that was quite a scare you gave me.' As always, Nigel was by my bedside. He reached for my hand and kissed it gently. 'How are you doing?' he said, stroking my forehead. The lighting was fairly dim, but it was still light enough to see the tears welling up in Nigel's eyes. 'I'm sorry, bun,' I muttered. 'Hey, what for?' he questioned.

'All this mess,' I snuffled.

'Don't be silly, I just want you better,' he smiled. 'Rest now'.

Apart from the Septicaemia being life-threatening, it's also made me very poorly and extremely weak for several weeks at a time. Unfortunately for me it wasn't the first and last time. I was terribly disappointed about Peru. Obviously, there was no way I would be well enough to travel, although I did contemplate it until Nigel and my surgeon said, 'No way, with a capital N.' It would have been suicide to do so. Although I never made it to Peru, I did manage to secure some alpacas from the ill-fated trip.

Six months in quarantine in Switzerland, and they would be allowed into the United Kingdom, but not until. I would just have to be patient. And patient I was, although I was lucky enough to have the opportunity to spend some time visiting the alpacas whilst in quarantine. As is usually required, Joy would have to make a trip out to Switzerland to oversee part of the quarantine process and, as luck would have it, Joy invited me to join her. I was thrilled and said, 'Yes' immediately. For me, that trip sealed our friendship. We just had a great time together; we shared our love of alpacas over evening meals, and talked into the early hours whilst sipping the occasional glass of red wine. That trip also taught me a great deal. Joy had arranged a team of various specialists to join us in Switzerland for certain processes that needed to be carried out with the alpacas. A vet was flown out from England along with a video cameraman; also a very well-renowned alpaca expert, called Eric Hoffman, was flown in from America. I'd read several of his books, so I was very excited at the thought of being able to meet and work with him. A lovelier man you couldn't wish to meet. After a couple of days we were all comfortable in each other's company; and boy, did we have some laughs! On one day we had an exceptionally early start. We knew we had loads of detailed quality grading to do with the alpacas, so when the going gets tough the tough get going. I'm not sure to this day what started Joy and I laughing, but it was one of those girly occasions when the two of us just did. The five of us (Joy, the three men and me) were loading the car with equipment for the day's work ahead, when we both started laughing, at what I don't know, but we did. We were holding our sides crying with laughter. The men stood like cardboard cut-outs staring at us in amazement; they just didn't get it. The more they stared, the more we laughed; we were debilitated with laughter that much that neither of us could climb in to the car. Anyway, we thought it was funny even though nobody else did!

Following that first bout of septicaemia I've had several more since, all of which have seen me hospitalised. The problem with this is that I was by then extremely susceptible to infection which, in turn, caused even more problems because of the farm work.

In the end it was decided that the best possible solution to all this was to place me on daily antibiotics. I wasn't particularly happy about this, but beggars cannot be choosers, and I thought if it keeps me out of hospital then so be it.

The number of people visiting the farm was increasing year upon year, and more often than not we were asked by visitors if there was anywhere to buy a coffee or drinks from on site. This got me thinking. I prepared a short survey asking visitors to complete what other facilities they might like to see at the farm. Over a period of months it was unanimous; a coffee shop was the answer. Armed with survey results, we applied to Sheffield City Council for planning consent to change an area of the barn into a coffee shop. Within weeks of the planning permission being granted we set out to have the coffee shop completed for the start of the summer season. As with all these deadlines it was a race to the finish. The Friday evening before we opened, Denise, Mark (my brother in law), Nigel and I were still desperately trying to put the final touches in place to enable us to open as planned the following day. Four very tired people locked the doors at 4.00am that Saturday morning. We opened our doors to the public five hours later on Saturday 3rd July 2006.

Baby Boom

Business was booming and so were babies. Well, I actually mean cria's (baby alpacas). This particular year saw thirty-five cria being born. I'd been involved with these wonderful creatures now for eight years.

Eight years on and my life was looking very different. The success that business brought me enhanced my confidence considerably. Throughout my life I'd been a relatively quiet person. I didn't like confrontation, my self esteem was extremely low, and I didn't feel that my opinion was of any interest to anyone. Nigel would get frustrated at me doubting myself all the time. Almost every decision I tried to make would involve asking Nigel if he thought I was making the right decision.

Now, though, I was beginning to find I had a voice, a voice that people actually wanted to hear. I can remember being amazed that people/customers wanted my opinion and advice on alpacas. That in itself I just couldn't comprehend. I'd always been the needy one. Suddenly I was beginning to realise that yeah, probably I might have some self worth after all. I was in demand for speaking at 'after dinner presentations' to various groups, something of which I never thought in a million years I would be capable of pulling off, let alone confident of doing.

I can remember one particular occasion. It was a Saturday evening. Garry was a colleague of Nigel's, and his wife had been diagnosed with breast cancer three years earlier. Jean and Garry were very sympathetic to our situation, having experienced it first-hand. When I arrived home from hospital there was the most beautiful bouquet of flowers at our front door; they were from Garry and Jean. From then on Jean rang me on several occasions; I enjoyed our chats. This particular Saturday evening Nigel had persuaded me to meet up with them for drinks and dinner at a local country restaurant. Reluctantly I agreed, but that evening was the start of me being my true self. I was sick of putting different hats on to suit different people at different times. I decided that I would have my half of bitter instead of the Gin and tonic that I thought a young lady should choose. I was going to be me whether they liked me or not; I would be true to myself no matter what the consequences. At times I do tend to say and do ridiculous things, but that's just me. As Nigel has always said to me, 'Elaine, just be yourself and people will love you for who you are.' I know this may sound rather simplistic to most people, but throughout my life this had been a real issue for me, I never thought I was good enough. Not any more though. The tides were a-changing.

Due to the workload of running a growing breeding herd of alpacas, plus a coffee shop single-handed, it was proving very stressful. My on-going health problems didn't help the situation either. I started experiencing minor dizzy spells, but over a number of weeks the so called 'dizzy spells' were extending in time. Sometimes it was a matter of hours before I could focus properly again. I can only explain the feeling as being light-headed, pretty much how you sometimes feel when you've had one too many! Nigel was convinced that we needed medical advice. Denise, my sister, worked at the Royal Hallamshire Hospital as a secretary to an ear, nose and throat consultant. Fortunately, she was able to get me an out-of-hours consultation, which proved rather enlightening. Hours of tests took place to determine what the various conditions could be. The outcome was that the common condition was diagnosed as acute stress! 'Stress': I always thought that was a polite way of meaning 'unable to cope', and I suppose I just couldn't. Looking back now though, I'm surprised I 'coped' as well as I did for as long as I did.

In essence, I was running two separate businesses. The prognosis was that the dizzy spells would worsen, plus added complications, if I didn't change my lifestyle: and quickly. I immediately took this as a sign of failure. I desperately didn't want to fail, but the truth of the matter was that I could only run one of the businesses competently. Reluctantly, I agreed with Nigel that the sensible option was to advertise the coffee shop for lease. Again, looking back it was the right decision. I realised soon afterwards that my one passion had always been working hands-on with the alpacas. Over a period of weeks the dizzy spells lessened until they seemed to just drift away and peace was restored once more.

It was round about this time that I met Fred. Fred was the husband of the lady who leased the coffee shop, Lesley. Most weekends Fred would help Les out in the coffee shop. It was a busy little place, especially in summertime, so an extra pair of hands was always welcome. Quite often Fred would wander out onto the farm to see what jobs Rachael and I were doing. Rachael was my one member of staff helping on the farm at that time. One particular afternoon, Rachael and I had run some stud males down from one of the far paddocks. Bearing in mind we have forty-two acres, you can appreciate the farm is spread out over quite a large area. Far Ringinglow paddock, as we refer to it, gives you a clue as to where it is in relation to the farm building.

Roughly every three months, we trim all the herd's toenails. The studs were the only group left to do, so I decided that in the two hours we had available, that would be a good job to complete before the end of the day. The studs had other ideas. The farm building and surrounding area had been designed by Nigel, so it was very well thought out; ease of use was a priority. All our home paddocks could be accessed and worked so that animals could be run back and forth to 'catch pens' by just one person. All my alpacas are 'well handled', and familiar with my voice and those of my staff, so it's never been a problem calling them towards the myriad of gates we have accessing the different paddocks. Alpacas are extremely intelligent creatures and are very quick to learn.

In the early years, I brought all my alpacas into the barn during winter nights. Sometimes a paddock of animals would be split into two separate pens in the barn overnight. Over a period of nights, each alpaca instinctively familiarised themselves with their allocated pens and quite happily organised themselves, peeling off to their designated pens. How smart is that? For some bizarre reason, this particular afternoon the studs just didn't want to co-operate. Fred was stood nearby watching this little fiasco take place. When he offered his brawn to assist, I gratefully accepted. After a brief explanation on how to restrain an alpaca, Fred proudly strode into the catch pen to prove his masculine prowess. Warrior, the alpaca who stood opposite him, hummed loudly and looked him up and down with a knowing look. Fred stepped towards Warrior and commented, 'Now then, Warrior, you won't get the better of me, so let's be a good lad, eh?' Immediately that his outstretched arm made contact around Warrior's neck Fred was catapulted over the post-and-rail fence into the adjacent catch pen!

A surprised Fred struggled to his feet, with his glasses barely intact, diagonally across his face. With pursed lips and a smile I lightened the situation and quipped, 'Oh, yeah, I can see you've got a handle on him Fred.'

From that day on it was the beginning of a wonderful working relationship between Warrior and Fred... only joking, between Fred and me!

Since that day we became firm friends, and have remained so ever since.

Friends

On holiday in Jersey with our best friends Jane and Steve. August 2014

I liken friends to seasons of the year - they come and go. Some friends are lifelong friends but I would say they are only in the minority. That is the case for me anyway. My only lifelong friend, apart from my sister, is Bev. We've been friends for 47 years; we were both three years of age when we met. Bev is seven months older than me and, as far back as I can remember, was always a girly girl. I, on the other hand, was more of a tomboy. I hated wearing dresses, always preferring to wear dungarees like little boys, or a pair of shorts. I loved my toy gun and holster, with my paper caps making noises as if I were firing a bullet. Bev would shake her head at me when I wanted to play at football, instead preferring to play hop-scotch or something similar.

Both our families lived on Manvers Road, actually only five doors apart. We went to Sunday school together, and were always partnered up for Mayday shows, whether we were singing or dancing. On one occasion, I can remember we were re-enacting the 'Owl and the Pussycat' scene. Bev, being taller than me, was playing the part of the owl, and I being the smaller one was playing the part of the pussycat. All was going well until the artificial boat, that we were being pulled across the stage in, careered down a gulley where all the stage lights were positioned. The poor guy pulling the particular rope in question was horrified to see us disappearing off the scenery and down into the stage lights. Apart from the lights being fairly warm, Bev and I saw the funny side of it, thought it was great fun, and couldn't stop laughing. Good job it was only the dress rehearsal! What it is to be young! Although we were two very different children, they say opposites attract, and Bev and me certainly did that. In fact we were soul mates, and I'm sure we will remain friends until the day we die.

Funnily enough, I never made any real lasting friendships at school. I'm not sure why, possibly because I was so wrapped up with my athletics.

It wasn't until my working life that I made another close girlfriend. Carol also worked in the fines and fees department. Our desks were adjacent and so, over the years, we formed quite a close bond. Sadly, as I mentioned early in my book, Carol died at the age of just fifty-one from a reoccurrence of breast cancer. I remember being very affected by Carol's death. She knew she was dying, and she planned her funeral down to the nth degree, stating exactly what funeral car her friends should travel in, in the procession. I still think of Carol quite often, and think how unfair life can be at times. She had a tough life. She always worked hard to provide the best for her two boys, and just when she was starting to enjoy life, it was so cruelly taken away from her. I suppose it's fair to say that I've been very fortunate to find some very good friends later on in life.

I met Cathy, who is also my hairdresser, within a few months of my first cancer op. At the time she was dating the brother of mutual friends of ours Trudi and Chris. Trudi and Chris ran a local pub/restaurant, and it was on one of these occasions that we first met. This particular evening the restaurant was very busy. Chris had already introduced us to his brother, Richard, earlier that evening. When Cathy joined us we hit it off immediately. In the end we decided to share a table and we are still good friends to this day. In those early days of my recovery, I tended to get inebriated fairly quickly. I was going to say it was probably down to the drugs I was taking but, actually, if I'm being totally honest, it probably wasn't anything to do with that. The truth of the matter was that I was only just finding myself as a person. I was enjoying being me, and I was enjoying being amongst friends. Consequently I tended to over-indulge a little too much. It was a sort of freedom thing. Bless them, so many times poor Cathy and Trudy have held my head whilst I've been sick in the ladies toilets. They've held my hand and cleaned me up and then, the following week I'd do it all again! By the way, I must just add that those occurrences were relatively short-lived, just until I came to my senses! What a crazy time in my life, but hey, that's what I call good friends.

We've had so many good times, with so many good friends, and hopefully many more times to come. Tony and Sue live in our local village, own an apartment in Spain and, in fact, it was Tony and Sue who first introduced us to a lovely part of Spain, when they invited us to stay with them for a week's holiday. What a holiday we had. We partied into the early hours, and danced the nights away. What a blast we had, and yes, we still do! In my quieter moments, maybe one would say mellow moments, I can look back, and feel sorry that some friendships have not stood the test of time. Joy, and David, Trish, and John, for whatever reasons, it doesn't really matter. There is, however, one criterion that does matter though, and that is bitterness, and recriminations, and I bear none of them. Life is just far too short.

It must be ten years ago since we first met Jane and Steve. It was a chance meeting really, at an even more unusual occasion: a mutual friend's son's Indian wedding. Not having ever experienced such an occasion before, we didn't know what to expect at all. It was certainly an eye-opener. On arrival, all the ladies were sent into a room on the left hand side of a corridor, the men on the right. It was here where I first made Jane's acquaintance. Being the only other white face in the room, we were immediately drawn towards each other. It was strange because I felt like I'd met her somewhere before. I hadn't, of course, but conversation flowed so easily. Shortly afterwards, our conversation was halted by being escorted out of the room, where we were asked to stand in an orderly queue. The men were in the room opposite and were asked to do the same. As we stood there, I quietly whispered to Jane about who Nigel was stood with. 'That's Nigel, stood talking to the chap with the bald head'. 'Really?, she replied. 'Because that's my husband'. The remainder of the afternoon/ evening was spent chatting, and swapping stories and, of course, the occasional alcoholic beverage! The strange thing was, that night neither of us exchanged phone numbers, which was odd considering we'd all got on so well.

Ironically, it wasn't until three years later that our paths crossed once more, but this time we did exchange contact details. From that day forward, our friendship has grown, not just as two girlfriends, but also as four friends who just enjoy each other's company. There are so many similarities that we all share. As two couples, we were both married in June 1988, Steve and Jane on the eleventh, and Nigel and me on the eighteenth. The weird coincidence was that we wanted to get married on the eleventh June also, the number eleven has always been my lucky number, and it was also my Star Walk number. Unfortunately for us, the church was available on the eleventh, but not the reception venue; hence having to go with the eighteenth. My sister, Denise, shares the same birthday with Jane's brother, the tenth of February, and our mums were both aged forty when they gave birth to us. Weird! But true.

'You certainly find out who your true friends are' is a cliché, I know, but a very accurate one, and one that I've heard used on many occasions, by many different people. Steve and Jane have been the most loyal of friends. They've held out the hand of friendship to me when I've needed them most, and to Nigel, when he's needed their support. Mental illness is a difficult one to deal with for everyone; you can't put a plaster on it to make it better, it's not that easy. However, they've shown patience, understanding and affection, but above all, they're 'just there for both of us'.

To both Jane and Steve, my heartfelt thanks.

Grand Triathias Grandslam

'Grand Triathias Grand Slam' (Nimbus) my new boy

Being hands-on with my animals has always been the most enjoyable part of running my own business. However, riding Prince was another one of my passions and, although I didn't find as much time as I would have liked to ride, he was still a big part of my life. Recently though, I was becoming more and more concerned about the amount of times Prince was seemingly falling lame. On a number of occasions he'd seem fine one day, and the next he would be terribly lame. Having been around horses for a number of years now, I was aware that at certain times in their life a horse may become lame for no known reason. Prince on the other hand had always been quite a stoic horse and never really had much lameness; this however was not the case recently. On several occasions I'd called my vet out to look into

Prince's situation. Prince and I had been a partnership now for twelve years, and I new him pretty well. My instincts told me something just seemed very wrong. After a series of in-depth tests I received the news that I just didn't want to hear. It was confirmed that he had a degenerate disease of his coffin joints in both his front feet.

Nothing is ever straightforward with animals. I was receiving conflicting opinions on how best to deal with this problem and, by the time I'd completed my own research, I was only further confused. In the end I made the only decision possible with Prince's best interests at heart. I would retire him, and keep him in the luxury to which he had become accustomed. He deserved only the best. He had served me well. He had always looked after me, and now it was time for me to do the same for him. He would spend his days, and ultimately end his days, with me, relaxing in retirement in his home paddocks.

I felt good that I'd done the best for Prince. However, I now found myself creating another dilemma. I was forty-seven, but I felt a young forty-seven at that. I was healthy, strong and still had plenty of ambitions but, and it was a big but, I had no horse to ride. I was offered various horses to ride from my livery clients and, although I accepted their kind offers, I found myself once again yearning to have my own personal horse to ride. As always when I'm unsure, I turn to Nigel to talk over my thoughts; this time was no exception. Cathy, a good friend of mine, has always joked with me saying, 'Elaine, whatever you want you get when you ask Nigel; you can wrap him round your little finger.' This time was no exception. The search was on for another horse! I tried to be sensible, taking into consideration my age, and what type of horse I thought I could and couldn't handle. I thought about it for a while, and then threw the 'SENSIBLE' out of the window! I decided to go with my heart and not with my head. Sure enough, a few weeks later I laid eyes on what I believed may be my next equestrian partner, he came in the form of a stunning fifteen hands one inch black Welsh section D cob. The advertisement showed video footage of him competing in both dressage and cross-country; I thought he looked awesome in the way he moved.

I wasted no time and, after a twenty minute phone conversation with the present owner, I had made all the arrangements to make the three-and-a-half hour car journey down to Hampshire the following week to try him out. After placing down the receiver I smiled to myself, and was even more convinced that I might have found the right one. I was excited, very excited in fact. Nigel booked us in at 'The Potters Heron Hotel'. It was and still is a hotel that we frequent often when travelling in that area of the country and, considering it would be late afternoon by the time we would be finished in Hampshire, Nigel thought it would make sense to stay overnight at the Potters. It was a good excuse anyway.

Grand Triathias Grandslam was his show name, and he certainly looked 'showy'.

He was every bit what I had imagined he would be. My initial thoughts were how well he stood. He looked strong and capable, he had good legs and back, and his black native mane looked stunning as it swayed gently in the morning sunshine.

Sarah, his owner, was shortly due to emigrate to New Zealand to start a new life. Apart from her mum she had no other family ties to remain in the UK, and her dream had always been to relocate to sunnier climes. The move was imminent, so it was really important for her to find a loving home for her precious boy. I'd asked Sarah if she would ride him for me first in the ménage so I could see him put through his paces. Again, he didn't disappoint. Sarah had obviously worked hard in the past bringing his schooling on and I could clearly see that he had far more potential to shine in the future. I decided there and then that, if he performed as well when I hacked him out, I wanted his future to be part of my future as his new owner. It was difficult to contain my excitement when Sarah put him over a series of jumps; it was like watching poetry in motion. It also occurred to me that if he had such an obvious passion for fences then maybe, just maybe, my ambition to compete in a cross-country course might just be plausible. 'Steady Elaine, steady,' I thought to myself, 'let's not carried away.' But of course I did, so much so that I was virtually writing the cheque out. Slipping my foot into the stirrups felt like slipping my foot into a comfy pair of slippers, he was just what I had been looking for. Sarah had arranged to borrow her mum's horse so we could hack out together, which I was pleased about because I didn't know the area at all. With my sense of direction I would surely have got lost... even with directions! The hack confirmed my decision. Grand Triathias Grandslam would be my next horse if I could secure the deal.

And I did!

Menagerie

Over the following years the number of alpacas increased, and so did the rest of my animal collection. My alpaca herd now totalled one hundred and twenty five animals, plus three llamas. Bodie and Doyle, my cats, and the 'Three Amigos', as I lovingly referred to my three dogs, Bracken a black Labrador, Bramble a yellow Labrador and Chico my long haired Chihuahua.

I had also somehow managed to collect forty-two ducks, two geese, fifteen chickens, seven goats, one Kune Kune pig, two micro pigs, two turkeys, twelve sheep, and my two wonderful horses Prince and Nimbus (yard names). Not bad, hey? Oh, and by the way, six horses on livery. I was forty-seven, and in 2010 Nigel was nearing his half century. Nigel had always said that he wanted to retire at the age of fifty and, unbelievably, that time was rapidly approaching. Nigel had broached with me the possibility of me retiring at the same time but, being nearly four years his junior, I was adamant that I was too young to retire. Apart from anything else I didn't feel ready. However, Nigel was more than ready. He'd been running his own business for thirty-three years, and was looking forward to the prospect of an easier and more relaxing lifestyle. Reaching your half-century is quite a milestone in anyone's life so, with that in mind, we decided that it should be marked with a celebration and, of course, Nigel was also retiring, so it was a double celebration. The venue was one of our favourites: a small Italian restaurant, which we frequented quite often. In fact, the restaurant is so small that I rented out the complete first floor. Everyone had a fantastic evening; we even carried on the party back at our house until the early hours.

The farm was by now very well-established. It had expanded beyond recognition and, as with all businesses, the bigger the company the bigger the concerns. I was beginning to experience some of the pitfalls first hand. My staffing levels had obviously needed to increase, and my feed bills had also increased dramatically, as well as the variety of feedstuffs for the different species that I now owned. Considering I had always imagined Mayfield Alpacas to remain a relatively small concern, it was increasing at quite an alarming rate. I can remember the reality almost struck me overnight. Fred was now employed full-time on the farm, and it wasn't long before he became my right hand man, with the title 'yard manager'. I suppose over the years I have tended to lean on Fred more and more. I respect Fred, and his opinion matters to me a great deal. I'm also a big believer in two heads being better than one. Without a doubt, we've certainly had our fair share of laughs along the way, and yes, we've had some tears.

The early autumn of 2012 saw the beginning of a farmer's worst nightmare!

The summer had been a very wet one, and the grass had struggled to grow in the volume we would normally expect. To make good haylage we needed three days of hot dry weather to cut, turn and bale the crop. Nigel constantly trawled the BBC five-day forecast looking for a fair-weather window in the damp, gloomy weather. Eventually the forecast predicted some sunshine, and we instructed our contractor to cut the crop. We were now committed! All seemed to be going well until the final day, when the crop had been baled, but was still yet to be wrapped. The first warning sign was the noticeable difference in the wind strength. As the breeze picked up the skies darkened. I glanced skyward and was immediately greeted with several droplets of rain falling onto my face. 'Oh no, not now,' I groaned. 'Please, not now'.

Half of the crop had by now been baled, half had not. Time was of the essence.

Once again the forecast had got it wrong. Lady luck was just not shining on us that day, and instead bad luck was. The heavens opened and, for the following two hours, boy did it rain! All in all it had been a frustrating day. On the one hand we were relieved to have finally completed the wrapping, but on the other hand we couldn't help wondering just how detrimental the decision to continue wrapping might be in the future. There was no way of knowing now. Only time would tell, and it certainly did. The winter started early that year. Bitter cold winds and rain constantly battered the counties, causing chaos and havoc in every corner of the country. Major damage was caused by catastrophic floods, hailed by some as the worst in living memory. People's lives were turned upside down by the freak weather conditions, just as I was about to experience the toughest and most heartbreaking six months of my farming career.

It was one day in October when it started. In the winter months I have always housed my girls in the barn at night; this year was to be no different. The boys, however, had wintered out in the paddocks for some years now, where they all had access to large, well-equipped field shelters.

My philosophy for this was that the majority of my girls would always be pregnant over the winter, so required a little more TLC. After all, the girls had to cope with:

a.   Being pregnant

b.   Growing a foetus

c.   Feeding a cria from the summertime

d.   Requiring much more feed and energy just to stay warm, let alone considering all what their bodies were coping with.

The barn is airy and well-ventilated, with a variable permeable membrane on the inside, providing the unique system of staying warm in winter but cool in summer. Perfect, it had worked well for the past sixteen years. Why then should I deem this year to be any different? The fact is I didn't.

Hard Knocks

Sadness and bad luck for me, as long as I can remember, come in the months October, November and December. I dread those months in advance. It's also inevitable with farming that when you have livestock you get dead stock, even if like me you do not farm on a commercial basis for meat. I would estimate on a yearly basis you may lose around 7% of your herd, less if you are fortunate, but 2012/2013 saw a terrible loss of alpacas for me. One by one my animals were becoming seriously ill, and I didn't understand why; to be honest, neither did the vets. The symptoms were loss of weight ultimately leading to emaciation, lethargy, difficulty in standing and then death. The situation continued throughout November and December, with more and more of my beloved alpacas dying.

For many of them I took the decision to end their suffering in the kindest way I could. This came in the form of a lethal injection to put them to sleep gently. I sat with every single one of them in my arms. Cradling them, I would stroke their faces and tell them that everything was going to be alright. I told them how much I loved them. I thanked them for saving me, and they responded by humming back to me. I kissed their faces while their beautiful eyes looked into mine. Their gorgeous eyelashes, almost damp with tears of their own, blinked a simple trust that I shall never forget as long as I live. 'Sleep well, my darling,' I whispered, and then they were gone. The thought of them being cut open for the post-mortem exam at the lab made me shudder. I couldn't even give them a dignified goodbye! It's difficult to describe, but the hurt and sadness I felt, and still do, goes far beyond what one would expect from the normal loss of one's pet.

No, it goes far, far deeper than that. They are in my soul and will remain there forever more.

On Saturday 7th January 2013 I received another massive blow. It was around 9.30 am. I was upstairs on the mezzanine floor preparing Bracken's and Bramble's breakfast, when the familiar tune of my mobile phone rang. I rummaged through the several layers of thermal clothing, before the person on the other end of the phone got fed up and put the receiver down. 'Damn the winter,' I thought to myself, as I pulled out my mobile. The screen on my mobile showed, 'Helen – vet' calling. Hurriedly, I pressed the recall button and waited anxiously for Helen to pick up. 'Hi, Helen, sorry about that, couldn't find my mobile quick enough'. As Helen spoke, I could feel a cold sweat sweeping through my body. I stood motionless, asking her to repeat what the latest implications meant. 'Elaine, I'm afraid I've got some worrying news from the lab. They've found some suspected TB lesions'. Forty minutes later I pressed the 'end' button on my mobile. I'd heard all I needed to know for now. I stared across the staff kitchen to where I'd walked, trying to comprehend what I had just been told: DEFRA, movement ban, possible herd cull. 'No, no, surely not? This can't be happening, not to me, not to my alpacas. I put their health before mine. I love them too much. There must be some mistake'. The irony of it though, was that it was happening to me and my alpacas. Tuberculosis is a chronic, granulomatous, bacterial, infectious disease, characterised by the development of tubercles (small avascular nodules containing giant cells) in various organs of the body. Recently, there has been an upsurge in cases, made particularly bad because many strains have become resistant to medication. It is a serious problem in immunocompromised individuals, (very similar to me with Lymphodemia and infection). Lesions are commonly found in the respiratory and digestive systems, and excretions and secretions may be contaminated with the organism. Infection may be acquired by inhalation or ingestion.

Three days later I received a letter of notification informing me of the 'movement ban' that had been enforced on my farm. Basically, I was restricted to the movement of animals on or off my farm for the foreseeable future. For me there was further agonising news in that we would have to wait fifty-six days for these suspicions to be confirmed. Apparently, TB takes a great length of time to be cultured; hence we had no choice but to sit and wait. The anxiety didn't stop there though. It seemed like every day we had another alpaca exhibiting similar symptoms. Most days I dreaded walking onto the farm in fear of what I might find, and I openly admit to purposely waiting until Fred arrived before me; it was heartbreaking. I owe so much to Fred over those very difficult six months. He was a real mate for me to lean on, and without his understanding and care I don't know how I would have coped. Fred was hurting too. I could see it in his eyes. He loved those animals like me, and they had become a part of his life. Over the years, Fred has joked with me and said, 'The only way you're going to get me off this farm is when you carry me out in my coffin.' Dear Fred, what a lovely man.

January came and went and so did the deaths. Oh, how I wished for those halcyon days when Mayfield Alpacas was in its infancy; it seemed all so easy back then.

Why was it all going wrong so quickly? I searched the internet and text books for any answers, any reasons. Surely I must have overlooked something fundamental.

I found nothing new and, more worryingly, even the vets were scratching their heads. In February the lab reported that two more alpacas had similar suspicious lesions. I was at the end of my tether. The doubts had already started to kick in. I started questioning my competence as an alpaca breeder; what in god's name was happening to my alpacas, my business, my self-esteem? Everything that I had worked so hard for over the past sixteen years seemed to be hanging in the balance. So many times I cried for my animals. It couldn't just end like this. This was not how it was meant to be. In sixteen months time I wanted to hand over to Andy to continue my dream. I wanted it so much, but I was so tired. Tired of fighting! How many more times would I have to fight for something in my life? The penny then dropped!!! If I wanted my dream to continue then I was going to have to fight again, I was going to have to fight again because, if I didn't, nobody else would. Yes, they had once saved my life and now I knew I had to save theirs.

Survival Of The fittest

Raising a glass on our 25th Wedding Anniversary in the Maldives
June 2013

It was now sixteen weeks since the death of my first alpaca, and the so-called experts were no nearer to coming up with any answers. My frustration was building, and I knew it would now be up to me to find a solution to this nightmare. I knew I couldn't do it on my own. I needed moral and technical support and there was nobody better to turn to than Nigel. Nigel approaches everything with an engineer's mind, and this problem was no exception. We knew the animals were losing weight, and we now knew that the worm burden was high on the majority of animals that had a post mortem exam. However, there is one defining factor that sets alpacas apart from most other animals when it comes to detecting worms and, as I will explain later, this proved to be crucial in our situation.

Meanwhile, we decided to look at this from a different angle. Nigel asked me to compile all the nutritional data sheets for the feed we were using. A friend of Nigel's, Steve Walker, who is a very successful dairy farmer, came to the farm one day, and it was whilst we were having coffee that I expressed my concerns to Steve. I knew Steve would be a good source of information. I respected him as a farmer, and in no way was I concerned that by involving Steve we might jeopardise our need for discretion with regard to suspected TB. Analysing the haylage that we had made the previous summer was another suggestion. Nigel assembled a large spreadsheet and, as we entered the data for the feed, together with the dietary information for alpacas, which we had researched from South American websites, a startling pattern started to appear. My animals, for the first time in sixteen years, had a protein and copper deficiency. Not only that, I had my suspicions that the alpacas may well have become resistant to the wormers I was administering. I was mortified. The quantity of feedstuffs we had been feeding was on a massive scale; how then could this have happened? When the analysis of the haylage came back, the pieces of the jigsaw puzzle started to slot in to place. I had also enlisted the help and advice of Claire Whitehead, who I first met when I was staying down in Oxfordshire at Joy's home. Claire is Joy's daughter, a veterinarian specialising in camelids, who worked at the Royal Veterinary College in London. Claire also took a camelid research fellowship under the world renowned camelid expert, Dr David Anderson, at the Ohio State University, treating an impressive fifteen hundred camelid patients per year. I had also researched in some depth the myriad of alternative wormers available; unfortunately there are no wormers that are currently licensed specifically for alpacas. However, as I mentioned earlier, there is one defining factor that sets alpacas apart from most other species when it comes to detecting worms. It is in the way in which a worm burden is diagnosed. It is absolutely imperative that the correct procedure is performed for identifying parasite eggs in camelids faeces. Generally, camelids may be clinically affected at lower levels of parasite infestation than many other farm animals. Claire recommends the optimal diagnostic method for identifying gastrointestinal parasite eggs and coccidia in Camelids – the Modified Stoll's test. The standard test - the McMaster's test, which is more commonly used, is inferior to the Modified Stoll's test in the sensitivity in which it detects the amount of eggs per gram. The Modified Stoll's test is sensitive down to five epg (eggs per gram), as opposed to the McMaster's test which is only able to pick up faecal egg counts down to one hundred epg, or fifty epg in some labs. Not only that: the Modified Stoll's test is better at picking up the larger eggs produced by some other parasites which produce a lower number of eggs than others. The main thing is that lower egg counts can be much more significant in alpacas, but may be missed by other diagnostic methods. The reason the Modified Stoll's test is better at detecting lower egg counts is because it incorporates double centrifugation and uses a concentrated sugar solution.

Now, armed with all the information and technical data, we formulated our plan, putting everything into practice that we had now learned. Nigel set about making a hanging animal crate, which enabled us to weigh every alpaca in the entire herd, along with a digital crane scale, which he had purchased from eBay. From here we were able to calculate the correct amount of wormer (by drench and injection) for each individual alpaca. Steve also suggested that we might consider incorporating a high protein feedstuff as part of our unique, but totally unorthodox, alpaca diet. Steve suggested calf weaner nuts, which contain 17% protein. I had never heard of anyone feeding these to alpacas, but we had nothing to lose and everything to gain so we went for it. Week by week we religiously performed the necessary treatments, along with the weekly weighing of the herd, which was recorded onto another of Nigel's excel spreadsheets. Three weeks in to the new feed regime and we were starting to see some incredible results. The alpacas had started gaining in weight, were obviously responding to the treatments, and generally looked in much better shape. I was overjoyed; we all were.

Nevertheless, we still had to wait for the final decision/results from DEFRA: would we have TB in the herd or not? Until then we couldn't rest on our laurels. It was an agonising wait, but the positive indication that I tried to focus on was that the alpacas were improving in every single circumstance. I hoped and prayed we would be in the clear. When the results finally came through we were nearing the end of June 2013. I recognised the voice on the phone immediately as the lady from DEFRA. On hearing the results I dropped to my knees and wept, 'Thank you, God, thank you, God,' I repeated over and over again. As luck would have it Nigel was at the farm that particular afternoon. Sam, who was working in the coffee shop, panicked when she saw me on my knees and alerted Nigel. He lifted me up and wrapped his arms around me as he had done so many, many times before, and through the muffled sobs I spurted out, 'Results are negative, they're negative.' All the anxiety, stress and worry of the past six months poured out like someone had opened a tap. Finally, finally it was all going to be okay. Nigel handed me his handkerchief as he wiped away my tears, and smiled.

For the first time in six months I truly believed that I would have a farm to handover, to handover to Andy and continue my dream!

My Baby – Handover

My best friend and sister Denise and Mark my brother-in-law with me supporting a 'Care for Cancer' fund raising evening. July 2013.

The day finally arrived. We had been talking about this day for fifteen months and it was now 'that day', Monday July 7th 2014. Tomorrow I would relinquish full control of my sixteen-year-old baby 'Mayfield Alpacas'. I cannot think of a word that comes close to describing how I felt. My whole body ached with the love I felt for my animals - the fear of letting go was so painful. Undoubtedly the decision, which we had made fifteen months ago, would ultimately change my life once again. Andrew Jonas would be the new face of Mayfield Alpacas. He had all the necessary credentials for the job: the qualifications, and the letters after his name, the experience and, apart from anything else, I really liked him as a person. I'd worked with Andy for nearly five years now, and I knew he was the right man for the job. It was time for me to move on and enjoy a more relaxed way of life with Nigel, family and friends. I know only too well, through bitter experience, that you only get one shot at life, it's certainly no dress rehearsal. Bringing Andy in would introduce young blood, new ideas and a fresh approach to the farm, and I knew Mayfield Alpacas was ready for that. I was getting tired. The past two winters had been hard work on the farm, and I couldn't keep working six days a week for much longer. Besides, I had other things to pursue, which I enjoyed: sailing, swimming, Nimbus and of course my menagerie. I decided to take one last walk around my farm with my dogs before I cleared my office. I knew I couldn't put it off for much longer.

Over the years I must have accumulated quite a lot of stuff. I was donating most of the stationary cupboard to Andy, but somehow I still managed to fill several boxes with personal memorabilia. My coloured Labrador figurines had stood on my desk for most of the time, along with my wooden alpaca, which had been a present from a customer in the early days of business. Where had those days gone? Sixteen years had passed so quickly. I picked up the figurines and wooden alpaca, and gently pressed them against my lips, closing my eyes to reminisce. These animals had been my lifeline when I needed them most. The tears welled up, and then came easily. I felt my legs go weak, and all the tension and apprehension of the past few weeks flooded out like a tidal wave. Crying quietly, I slumped down into my black executive chair, which had been a present from Nigel's mum and dad, again when 'Mayfield Alpacas' was born. I wondered whether I could deal with this sensibly. I wasn't doing too well at the moment. I tried to console myself with the fact that this wasn't the end. After all, we would still own the farm, I would always have a say in major decisions and, of course, my horses would still be stabled at the farm. I'd still be spending a reasonable amount of time at the farm looking after Prince and Nimbus. I tried to think of the positive ways that this step back would make. In actual fact the positives far outweighed the negatives, and I would have the best of both worlds. I could dip in and dip out just as much as I liked, without the day-to-day hassle that running your own business brings. Taking all this into account, why then didn't I feel convinced?

After a while I heard footsteps coming up the stairs. The sound of the voice was familiar, 'Hello, Hazel, where are you? Bruv here.' It was Mark, my brother-in-law. Mark very rarely calls me Elaine; instead he prefers to use my middle name Hazel. Likewise I refer to Mark as Bruv, and I suppose for both of us it's a kind of endearment term. Quickly, I tried to pull myself together. The pretence didn't last for long though, as Mark saw straight through it when he looked at my face! My once warm, colourful office of animal paintings and photographs now looked bare and empty. It looked representative of how I was feeling inside, and I know Mark felt it too. At five feet five inches, my small frame is dwarfed by Mark's size and height, towering above me at six feet five inches, but Mark is a gentle giant and, when he opened his arms inviting me for a cuddle, I accepted warmly, and we gently cried together.

Mark stayed with me for a while, but then once again I was alone with my own solitary thoughts. In preparation for the handover several weeks earlier, I'd composed a letter to send to friends, contacts and suppliers, informing them of the forthcoming changes at Mayfield that would take place on the 8th July 2014: one of which was my new email address. I would no longer be esharp@mayfieldalpacas.com. This, I found, was the first significant move to letting go. The final paragraph read: 'I'm sure you will all join me in wishing Andy all the luck in the world to attain his dream. I've certainly attained mine.' I re-read the draft letter out to Nigel to ask his opinion, but I failed miserably and broke down in tears before completing the paragraph. Nigel as always was there for me, insisting it was purely a new beginning: not the end.

Dear Fred, what a brick he'd been for me over the years. He'd broken my thoughts when he handed me a cup of tea saying, 'Come on, young lady, how about I help you load your car and then you can get off home?' Biting my lip I nodded and said, 'Thanks, Fred.'

I've never been very good at goodbyes, but today the 'Goodbyes' seemed somehow so final.

I had parked 'Dennis', my trusty Land Rover Defender, in the ménage so I could easily load up any personal stuff that I wanted to take home; but, to me, even 'Dennis' looked forlorn. Jacquie sat quietly sipping a cup of tea on one of the picnic benches outside the coffee shop. She was all too aware that this was a tough day for me. We'd grown pretty close over the past three years since we'd met up again. Jacquie would be part of Andy's new team. Jacquie and myself go back a long way. We had met some thirty-four years earlier, when we both worked in the fines and fees department at the Sheffield Magistrates Court. Jacquie worked in the 'enforcement section' of the office, and I in the 'cashiers section'. Our paths had then crossed once again when, three years ago, Jacquie and her husband John had visited the farm with their youngest daughter Emily. They became weekly visitors. Then one week Jacquie asked if it would be possible for Emily to volunteer, working at the farm on Saturdays. Emily was a nice kid and I warmed to her immediately. She reminded me very much of myself at her age. She had an obvious passion for animals and was prepared to get stuck in and work hard to learn her trade. The only problem was that she was under age to work alone on the farm without being accompanied by an adult. Jacquie happily said she would accompany 'Em' and offered her help as a volunteer as well. Never looking a gift horse in the mouth, I accepted gratefully - spare pairs of hands on the farm were always welcome. Since that day Jacquie has worked unreservedly without fail and has continued to do so even when Em came of age to work independently.

By December 2013, Jacquie and Andy had built up quite a rapport working alongside each other. Jacquie had helped out in the coffee shop when we were short-staffed, and this had obviously not gone unnoticed by Andy, bearing in mind that, in just six months time, he himself would be the one left holding the baby! Discussions obviously took place between the two of them and, when Jacquie finally agreed to take on the running of the coffee shop for Andy, I was really pleased for both of them. They would make a good team.

All loaded, I wandered back upstairs onto the mezzanine. Bracken and Bramble sat patiently on their mattress, waiting for their treat. They knew what was coming next, as it was a little ritual that happened every night, just before I left the farm. Tonight though was so very different. The farm looked different. My office looked different, and everything looked different. I needed to look around my office one more time before I finally closed the door, because tomorrow it wouldn't be my office any more. I thought about the times that I'd sat in that chair behind my desk so many times before: sometimes in sadness, sometimes in happiness. But what an incredible journey I'd travelled over the past sixteen years.

I owe my life to my animals. Without a shadow of a doubt, they have been my lifeline and my saviour. I took a deep breath, closed my eyes and pulled the door towards me. After all, closing the door was only closing another chapter, but hey, what a chapter! What indeed will the next chapter bring? Just watch this space!!!

Epilogue

Reflections

I never intended to turn my passion for alpacas into a business. It somehow just happened that way. Little Elaine Allen, from Manvers Road, running a thriving, successful business? It's impossible: that's what I would have said. To this day I sometimes have to pinch myself. When I look back over the past sixteen years, I feel privileged to have found my vocation in life with these wonderful creatures. I wonder how many people do! Back then the diagnosis of cancer turned my life upside down, and that of my family; but even in the blackest moments of despair there is always hope if you search for it. You just need the courage. Not that I realised it then, but it was the best thing that could have happened to me, for me personally that is. I was one of the lucky ones.

What next for me then? Well, now it's eight weeks on from handover, and it's all still very strange.

To be honest, I'm not quite sure where I fit in just yet. I suppose I feel a little bit like a nomad, wandering around aimlessly. However, I'm sure that's only temporary. What I am able to do is enjoy Nimbus. I plan to bring him back into work slowly, and hopefully, over the next few weeks, we will both become comfortable in our new roles. Of course, I now have the time to spend some quality time with my beloved alpacas and indeed, all my other animals. Our exotic species are rapidly increasing. New enclosures have been designed and erected: internally and externally. Our meerkats have just had babies, and our wallabies, Shane and Bruce, have settled in really well, as have the chinchillas, chipmunks, ferrets, guinea pigs, finches, oh and our two skunks! Certainly, some exciting times ahead for all of us. I personally cannot think of anyone more caring and capable than Andy to take my farm to the next level. I'm confident that my baby is in safe hands, and I wish Andy all the luck in the world to reach his dream. Here's to Sheffield's first zoo!

Finally, for everyone who has read my book, I hope you will believe that anything is possible if you really want it badly enough. Never, never give in, and remember always, 'Fight for your Dream'.

Lightning Source UK Ltd.
Milton Keynes UK
UKOW04f1921050615

252993UK00001B/10/P